4·95

Sing to God

Sing to God

Christian Songs for Juniors

compiled by
Margaret V. Old and
Elspeth M. Stephenson

Scripture Union
130 City Road, London EC1V 2NJ

ACKNOWLEDGMENTS

We would like to thank the following people for their help : Mrs. Jennifer Baker, A.R.C.M., G.R.S.M. ; Miss Sally Breeze ; Mr. D. J. Crawshaw, G.R.S.M. ; Mr. Alan Durden, B.A. ; Mr. Alastair Durden, B.Mus., F.R.C.O. ; Mr. Michael Ellis ; Rev. M. J. H. Fox, B.D. ; Mr. Patrick Harrex, B.A. ; Mrs. L. Taylor, B.Com. The items have been arranged for guitar by Frank H. Ferrett, B.Tech.

COPYRIGHT

USE WITH GUITAR

We hope these hymns, songs and choruses will be enjoyed to the accompaniment of various instruments. They have been arranged for guitar and all the chords used in the book are set out overleaf.
N.B. The suggested chords above each stave may not always be identified with the simultaneous piano chords.

So that the maximum use may be made of the songs by guitar players, the arrangements have been kept as simple as possible, the use of the capo being suggested for several items.

ISBN 0 85421 302 3 (Cased Edition)
ISBN 0 85421 547 6 (Limp Edition)

Printed and Bound in Great Britain by Purnell and Sons (Book Production) Ltd., Paulton, Bristol

CONTENTS

GUITAR CHORDS USED IN THIS BOOK

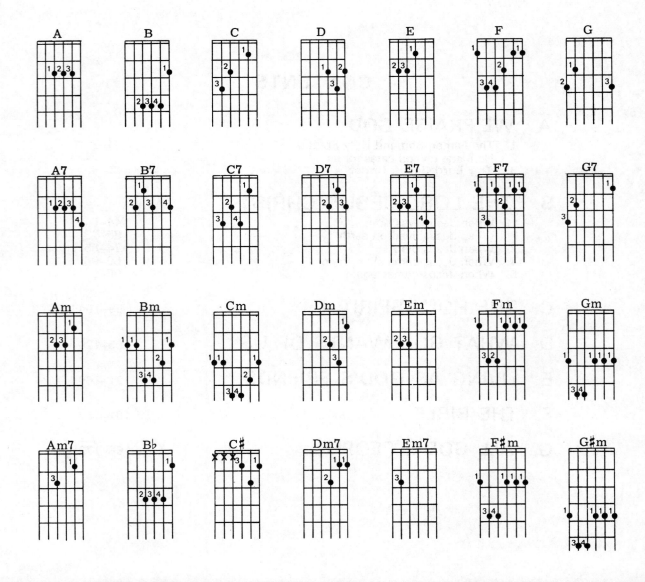

A. WE PRAISE GOD
1. The Father, Son and Holy Spirit

1. Praise God

Words: T. Ken (d. 1711)

Music: LASST UNS ERFREUEN Geistliche Kirchengesang
(Cologne 1623) arr. and harm. R. Vaughan Williams
(1872–1958)

Capo behind 1st fret

Praise God from whom all blessings flow,
Praise Him all creatures here below :
Alleluya ! Alleluya !
Praise Him above, ye heavenly host,
Praise Father, Son and Holy Ghost.
Alleluya ! Alleluya !
Alleluya ! Alleluya ! Alleluya !

Music from 'The English Hymnal' by permission of Oxford University Press

2. Praise Him, praise Him

To be sung as a round, unaccompanied

Praise Him, praise Him,
Praise Him in the morning,
Praise Him all the day.
Praise Him, praise Him,
Praise Him till the sun goes down.

3. Holy, holy, holy

Words: R. Heber (d. 1826)

Music: NICAEA   J. B. Dykes (d. 1876)
TERSANCTUS G. F. J. Hartless

1st tune NICAEA

1. Holy, holy, holy, Lord God Almighty!
   Early in the morning our song shall rise to Thee:
   Holy, holy, holy, merciful and mighty,
   God in three Persons, blessed Trinity!

2. Holy, holy, holy! All the saints adore Thee,
   Casting down their golden crowns around the glassy sea;
   Cherubim and Seraphim falling down before Thee,
   Who wert, and art, and ever more shalt be.

3. Holy, holy, holy! Though the darkness hide Thee,
Though the eye of sinful man Thy glory may not see;
Only Thou art holy, there is none beside Thee
Perfect in pow'r, in love and purity.

4. Holy, holy, holy, Lord God Almighty!
All Thy works shall praise Thy name, in earth, and sky, and sea;
Holy, holy, holy, merciful and mighty,
God in three Persons, blessed Trinity!

2nd tune TERSANCTUS

Capo behind 3rd fret

A. WE PRAISE GOD
2. He made us and cares for us
4. He's got the whole world in His hands

Music: Arr. D. J. Crawshaw

He's got the whole wide world _____ in His hands, He's got the

He's got the whole world

whole wide world _____ in His hands, He's got the whole wide world _____

He's got the whole world

He's got the

1. He's got the whole wide world in His hands,
   He's got the whole wide world in His hands,
   He's got the whole wide world in His hands,
   He's got the whole world in His hands.

2. He's got ev'rybody here, in His hands,
   He's got ev'rybody here, in His hands,
   He's got ev'rybody here, in His hands,
   He's got the whole world in His hands.

3. He's got the tiny little baby, in His hands,
   He's got the tiny little baby, in His hands,
   He's got the tiny little baby, in His hands,
   He's got the whole world in His hands.

4. He's got you and me brother, in His hands,
   He's got you and me sister, in His hands,
   He's got you and me brother, in His hands,
   He's got the whole world in His hands.

5. It is not just the moon we seek

Words: P. Lee

Music: Alfred B. Smith

It is not just the moon we seek,
It's the God who put it there.
Through Christ His Son He made the earth,
The sea, the sky, the air.
He sent His Son to take away
All fear of sin's dark power.
I will not fear, for Jesus will
Be with me every hour.

6. All creatures of our God and King

Words: St. Francis of Assisi
Tr. W. H. Draper

Music: LASST UNS ERFREUEN Geistliche Kirchengesang
(Cologne 1623) arr. and harm. R. Vaughan Williams
(1872–1958)

Capo behind 1st fret

1. All creatures of our God and King,
   Lift up your voice and with us sing;
   Hallelujah, Hallelujah!
   You burning sun with golden beam,
   You silver moon with softer gleam.

   Chorus: O praise Him, O praise Him,
   Hallelujah, Hallelujah, Hallelujah!

2. You rushing wind that is so strong,
   You clouds that sail in heav'n a-long,
   O praise Him, Hallelujah!
   You rising morn in praise rejoice,
   You lights of evening find a voice:
   Chorus:

3. You flowing water, pure and clear,
   Make music for your Lord to hear,
   Hallelujah, Hallelujah!
   You fire so masterful and bright,
   That gives to man both warmth and light:
   Chorus:

4. Let all things their Creator bless,
   And worship Him in humbleness,
   O praise Him, Hallelujah!
   Praise, praise the Father, praise the Son,
   And praise the Spirit, Three in One.
   Chorus:

7. Praise, my soul, the King of heaven

Words: H. F. Lyte (d. 1847)

Music: PRAISE, MY SOUL   J. Goss (d. 1880)

Capo behind 2nd fret

1. Praise, my soul, the King of heaven;
   To His feet thy tribute bring.
   Ransomed, healed, restored, forgiven,
   Who like thee His praise should sing?
   Praise Him! Praise Him! Praise Him! Praise Him!
   Praise the everlasting King.

2. Praise Him for His grace and favour
   To our fathers in distress,
   Praise Him, still the same for ever,
   Slow to chide and swift to bless.
   Praise Him! Praise Him! Praise Him! Praise Him!
   Glorious in His faithfulness.

3. Father-like, He tends and spares us;
   Well our feeble frame He knows;
   In His hands He gently bears us,
   Rescues us from all our foes.
   Praise Him! Praise Him! Praise Him! Praise Him!
   Widely as His mercy flows.

4. Angels, help us to adore Him;
   Ye behold Him face to face;
   Sun and moon, bow down before Him,
   Dwellers all in time and space.
   Praise Him! Praise Him! Praise Him! Praise Him!
   Praise with us the God of grace.

8. All things bright and beautiful

Words: C. F. Alexander (d. 1895)

Music: ALL THINGS BRIGHT AND BEAUTIFUL
W. H. Monk (d. 1889) ROYAL OAK   Traditional
17th Century
Fine

1st tune ALL THINGS BRIGHT AND BEAUTIFUL

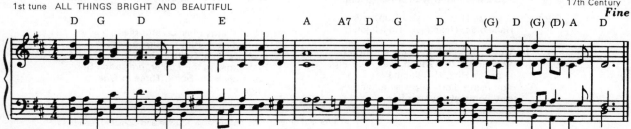

1. (and Chorus)
   All things bright and beautiful,
   All creatures great and small,
   All things wise and wonderful,
   The Lord God made them all.

2. Each little flower that opens,
   Each little bird that sings,
   He made their glowing colours,
   He made their tiny wings.
   Chorus:

3. The purple-headed mountain,
   The river running by,
   The sunset and the morning
   That brightens up the sky.
   Chorus:

4. The cold wind in the winter,
   The pleasant summer sun,
   The ripe fruits in the garden,
   He made them ev'ry one.
   Chorus:

5. He gave us eyes to see them,
   And lips that we might tell
   How great is God Almighty,
   Who has made all things well.
   Chorus:

2nd tune ROYAL OAK
Capo behind 1st fret

9. Praise the Lord! Ye heavens, adore Him

Words: Anon

Music: LAUS DEO   R. Redhead (d. 1901)

Capo behind 1st fret

1. Praise the Lord! Ye heavens, adore Him;
   Praise Him, angels in the height;
   Sun and moon, rejoice before Him;
   Praise Him, all ye stars and light.

2. Praise the Lord, for He hath spoken;
   Worlds His mighty voice obeyed;
   Laws, that never shall be broken,
   For their guidance He hath made.

3. Praise the Lord, for He is glorious;
   Never shall His promise fail;
   God hath made His saints victorious;
   Sin and death shall not prevail.

4. Praise the God of our salvation;
   Hosts on high His power proclaim;
   Heaven and earth, and all creation,
   Laud and magnify His name.

10. God is love: His the care

Words: P. Dearmer (d. 1936)

Music: THEODORIC Melody from
Piae Cantiones 1582
Arr. Gustav Holst (d. 1934) adpt.

Capo behind 1st fret

1. God is love: His the care,
   Tending each, everywhere.
   God is love—all is there!
   Jesus came to show Him,
   That mankind might know Him:

Chorus: Sing aloud, loud, loud!
   Sing aloud, loud, loud!
   God is good!
   God is truth! God is beauty! Praise Him!

2. None can see God above;
   All have here man to love;
   Thus may we Godward move,
   Finding Him in others,
   Holding all men brothers:
   Chorus:

3. Jesus lived here for men,
   Strove and died, rose again,
   Rules our hearts, now as then;
   For He came to save us
   By the truth He gave us:
   Chorus:

4. To our Lord praise we sing—
   Light and Life, Friend and King,
   Coming down love to bring,
   Pattern for our duty,
   Showing God in beauty:
   Chorus:

11. Let us with a gladsome mind

Words: J. Milton (d. 1674)

Music: MONKLAND   J. Antes
Arr. J. Wilkes (d. 1869)

Capo behind 1st fret

1. Let us with a gladsome mind
   Praise the Lord, for He is kind;
   Chorus: For His mercies shall endure,
                   Ever faithful, ever sure.

2. He, with all-commanding might,
   Filled the new-made world with light:
   Chorus:

3. All things living He doth feed,
   His full hand supplies their need:
   Chorus:

4. Let us, then, with gladsome mind,
   Praise the Lord, for He is kind!
   Chorus:

12. O worship the King

Words: R. Grant (d. 1838)

Music: HANOVER W. Croft (d. 1727)

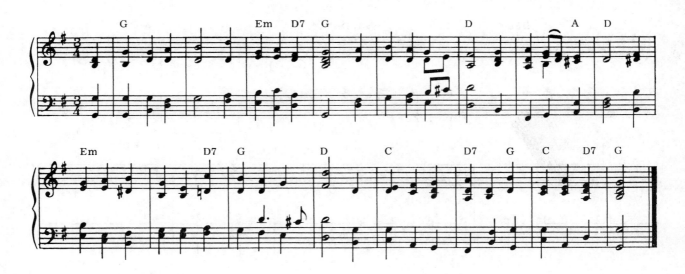

1. O worship the King,
   All-glorious above;
   O gratefully sing
   His power and His love:
   Our Shield and Defender,
   The Ancient of Days,
   Pavilioned in splendour
   And girded with praise.

2. O tell of His might,
   O sing of His grace,
   Whose robe is the light,
   Whose canopy space;
   His chariots of wrath
   The deep thunder-clouds form,
   And dark is His path
   On the wings of the storm.

3. The earth, with its store
   Of wonders untold,
   Almighty, Thy power
   Hath founded of old;
   Hath stablished it fast
   By a changeless decree,
   And round it hath cast,
   Like a mantle, the sea.

4. Thy bountiful care
   What tongue can recite?
   It breathes in the air,
   It shines in the light;
   It streams from the hills,
   It descends to the plain,
   And sweetly distils
   In the dew and the rain.

5. Frail children of dust,
   And feeble as frail,
   In Thee do we trust,
   Nor find Thee to fail;
   Thy mercies how tender,
   How firm to the end,
   Our Maker, Defender,
   Redeemer, and Friend!

13. God is good

Words: E. M. Nevill (1889–)

Music: ST. MABYN   A. H. Brown (d. 1926)

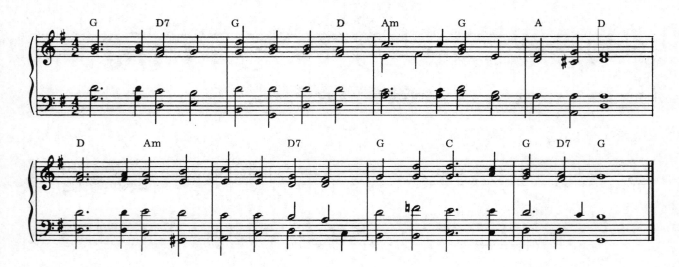

1. God is good, we come before Him,
   So that we may sing His praise;
   Giving thanks for all His goodness,
   As we learn His wondrous ways.

2. God is great, we come before Him,
   So that we may bow in prayer,
   Seeking strength to fight our battles,
   Knowing He is everywhere.

3. God is wise, we come before Him
   So that we may know His law,
   Learning from the men of old time
   How to serve Him more and more.

14. Let us praise God together

Words: J. E. Seddon

Music: CALHOUN MELODY   Arr. D. G. Wilson

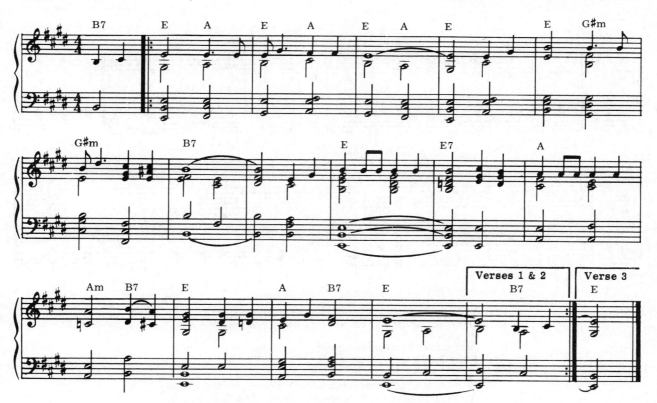

1. Let us praise God together,
   Let us praise;
   Let us praise God together
   All our days.
   He is faithful in all His ways,
   He is worthy of all our praise,
   His name be exalted on high.

2. Let us seek God together,
   Let us pray,
   Let us seek His forgiveness
   As we pray.
   He will cleanse us from all sin,
   He will help us the fight to win,
   His name be exalted on high.

3. Let us serve God together,
   Him obey;
   Let our lives show His goodness
   Through each day.
   Christ the Lord is the world's true light,
   Let us serve Him with all our might,
   His name be exalted on high.

15. Praise to the Lord

Words: J. Neander Tr. P Dearmer & C. Winkworth

Music: LOBE DEN HERREN
Stralsund Gesangbuch 1665

1. Praise to the Lord, the Almighty, the King of creation;
   O my soul, praise Him for He is thy health and salvation;
   All ye who hear,
   Brothers and sisters draw near,
   Praise Him in glad adoration.

2. Praise to the Lord, who doth prosper thy work and defend thee;
   Surely His goodness and mercy here daily attend thee;
   Ponder anew
   What the Almighty can do,
   If with His love He befriend thee.

3. Praise to the Lord! O let all that is in me adore Him!
   All that hath life and breath, come now with praises before Him!
   Let the Amen
   Sound from His people again;
   Gladly, for aye we adore Him.

16. God of concrete, God of steel

Words: R. G. Jones   Music: MINTERNE C. Taylor

1. God of concrete, God of steel,
   God of piston and of wheel,
   God of pylon, God of steam,
   God of girder and of beam,
   God of atom, God of mine,
   All the world of power is Thine.

2. Lord of cable, Lord of rail,
   Lord of motorway and mail,
   Lord of rocket, Lord of flight,
   Lord of soaring satellite,
   Lord of lightning's livid line,
   All the world of speed is Thine.

3. Lord of science, Lord of art,
   God of map and graph and chart,
   Lord of physics and research,
   Word of Bible, Faith of Church,
   Lord of sequence and design,
   All the world of truth is Thine.

4. God whose glory fills the earth,
   Gave the universe its birth,
   Loosed the Christ with Easter's might,
   Saves the world from evil's blight,
   Claims mankind by grace divine,
   All the world of love is Thine.

17. Now thank we all our God

Words: M. Rinkart Tr. C. Winkworth (d. 1878)

Music: GRACIAS G. Beaumont

1. Now thank we all our God,
   With hearts and hands and voices,
   Who wondrous things hath done,
   In whom His world rejoices;
   Who from our mother's arms
   Hath blessed us on our way
   With countless gifts of love,
   And still is ours today.

2. O may this bounteous God
   Through all our life be near us,
   With ever joyful hearts
   And blessed peace to cheer us;
   And keep us in His grace,
   And guide us when perplexed,
   And free us from all ills
   In this world and the next.

3. All praise and thanks to God
   The Father now be given,
   The Son, and Him who reigns
   With Them in highest heaven;
   The One eternal God,
   Whom earth and heaven adore;
   For thus it was, is now,
   And shall be evermore.

GRACIAS by permission of Paxton Music Ltd

18. Hundreds and thousands

Words: J. Gowans

Music: J. Larsson

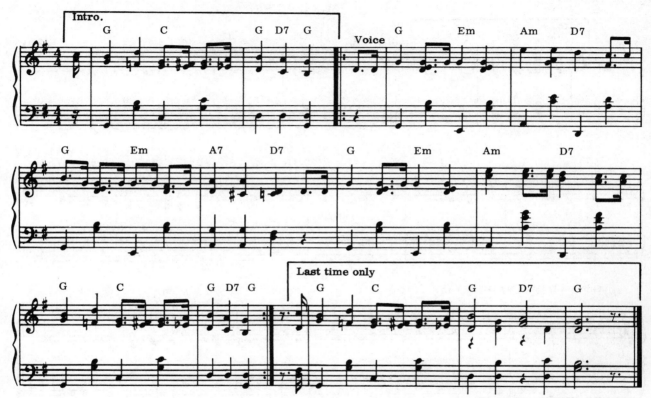

1. There are hundreds of sparrows, thousands, millions,
   They're two a penny, far too many there must be;
   There are hundreds and thousands, millions of sparrows,
   But God knows ev'ry-one and God knows me.

2. There are hundreds of flowers, thousands, millions,
   And flowers fair the meadows wear for all to see;
   There are hundreds and thousands, millions of flowers,
   But God knows ev'ry-one and God knows me.

3. There are hundreds of planets, thousands, millions,
   Way out in space each has a place by God's decree;
   There are hundreds and thousands, millions of planets,
   But God knows ev'ry-one and God knows me.

4. There are hundreds of children, thousands, millions,
   And yet their names are written on God's memory,
   There are hundreds and thousands, millions of children,
   But God knows ev'ry-one and God knows me!
   But God knows ev'ry-one and God knows me.

19. You can't stop God from loving you

Words: J. Gowans

Music: J. Larsson

1. You can't stop rain from falling down,
   Prevent the sun from shining,
   You can't stop spring from coming in,
   Or winter from resigning,
   Or still the waves or stay the winds,
   Or keep the day from dawning;
   You can't stop God from loving you,
   His love is new each morning.

2. You can't stop ice from being cold,
   You can't stop fire from burning,
   Or hold the tide that's going out,
   Delay its sure returning,
   Or halt the progress of the years,
   The flight of fame and fashion;
   You can't stop God from loving you,
   His nature is compassion.

3. You can't stop God from loving you,
   Though you may disobey Him,
   You can't stop God from loving you,
   However you betray Him;
   From love like this no pow'r on earth
   The human heart can sever,
   You can't stop God from loving you,
   Not God, not now, nor ever.

20. God who made the earth

Words: S. B. Rhodes (d. 1904)

Music: SOMMERLIED   H. von Muller

1. God who made the earth,
   The air, the sky, the sea,
   Who gave the light its birth,
   Careth for me.

2. God who made the grass,
   The flower, the fruit, the tree,
   The day and night to pass,
   Careth for me.

3. God who made the sun,
   The moon, the stars, is He
   Who when life's clouds come on,
   Careth for me.

4. God who sent His Son
   To die on Calvary,
   He, if I lean on Him,
   Will care for me.

21. When God made creation

Words: M. E. Rose

Music: NOW LET US HASTEN   M. Kruger

1. When God made creation,
   In true adoration
   The stars of the morning all shouted His praise:
   The sun in his splendour,
   The moon, young and tender,
   Sang: 'Praise to the Lord, the Ancient of Days.'

2. That God loved His children
   And happiness willed them,
   The stars and the beasts and the flowers knew well:
   But wilful man only,
   Preferred to be lonely,
   And turning from love, to darkness he fell.

3. But God would not leave him
   In sorrow and grieving,
   And came down to seek him in meekness and love.
   And gently He taught him,
   And dearly He bought him,
   And raised him again to glory above.

4. Then sing of God's glory,
   His wonderful story,
   O sing out His praise all you children of light;
   Through worlds never-ending,
   Your praises ascending:
   O sing of His love! O sing of His might!

22. Harvest

Words: J. Arlott

Music: SHIPSTON English Traditional Melody coll. Lucy Broadwood, harm. and arr. R. Vaughan Williams (1872–1958)

1. God, whose farm is all creation,
   Take the gratitude we give;
   Take the finest of our harvest,
   Crops we grow that men may live.

2. Take our ploughing, seeding, reaping,
   Hopes and fears of sun and rain,
   All our thinking, planning, waiting,
   Ripened in this fruit and grain.

3. All our labour, all our watching,
   All our calendar of care,
   In these crops of Your creation,
   Take, O God; they are our prayer.

23. We plough the fields

Words: M. Claudius (d. 1815)
Tr. J. M. Campbell (d. 1878)

Music: WIR PFLÜGEN   J. A. P. Schultz (d. 1800)

1. We plough the fields and scatter
The good seed on the land.
But it is fed and watered
By God's almighty hand;
He sends the snow in winter,
The warmth to swell the grain,
The breezes and the sunshine,
And soft refreshing rain;
Chorus : All good gifts around us
Are sent from heaven above;
Then thank the Lord,
O thank the Lord,
For all His love.

2. He only is the Maker
Of all things near and far;
He paints the wayside flower;
He lights the evening star;
The winds and waves obey Him;
By Him the birds are fed :
Much more to us, His children,
He gives our daily bread :
Chorus :

3. We thank You then, O Father,
For all things bright and good,
The seedtime and the harvest,
Our life, our health, our food.
No gifts have we to offer
For all Your love imparts,
But that which You desire most,
Our humble, thankful hearts :
Chorus :

24. Lord of the harvest

Words: F. Kaan

Music: Traditional Melody Arr. D. J. Crawshaw

1. We thank You, O God, for Your goodness,
For the joy and abundance of crops,
For food that is stored in our larders,
For all we can buy in the shops.

2. But also of need and starvation
We sing with concern and despair,
Of skills that are used for destruction,
Of land that is burnt and laid bare.

3. Then teach us, O Lord of the harvest,
To be humble in all that we claim,
To share what we have with the nations,
To care for the world in Your name.

A. WE PRAISE GOD
3. The Lord Jesus Christ
25. Come and praise

Words: Rev. Ian Bowman   Music: Traditional Arr. P. C. Butler and D. G. Wilson

Chorus :   Come and praise the Lord our King, Hallelujah,
            Come and praise the Lord our King, Hallelujah.

1.   Christ was born in Bethlehem, Hallelujah,
      Son of God and Son of Man, Hallelujah :
      Chorus :

2.   He grew up an earthly child, Hallelujah,
      Of the world, but undefiled, Hallelujah :
      Chorus :

3.   Jesus died at Calvary, Hallelujah,
      Rose again triumphantly, Hallelujah :
      Chorus :

4.   He will cleanse us from our sin, Hallelujah,
      If we live by faith in Him, Hallelujah.

      Chorus :

5.   We will live with Him one day, Hallelujah,
      And for ever with Him stay, Hallelujah :
      Chorus :

26. All glory, laud, and honour

Words: Theodulph of Orleans (c. 750–821)
Tr. J. M. Neale (d. 1866)

Music: ST. THEODULPH Melody by M. Teschner (c. 1615)
Harmony from J. S. Bach (d. 1750)

This hymn may be sung in six verses,
with verse 1 as chorus

1. All glory, laud, and honour
   To You, Redeemer, King,
   To whom the lips of children
   Made sweet hosannas ring !
   You are the King of Israel,
   You David's royal Son,
   Who in the Lord's name comes,
   The King and blessed One.

2. The company of angels
   Are praising You on high,
   And mortal men and all things
   Created make reply :
   The people of the Hebrews
   With palms before You went ;
   Our praise and prayer and anthems
   Before You we present ;

3. To You before Your passion
   They sang their hymns of praise ;
   To You now high exalted
   Our melody we raise :
   You did accept their praises ;
   Accept the prayers we bring,
   Who in all good delights,
   You good and gracious King.

27. Come, let us join our cheerful songs

Words: I. Watts (d. 1748)

Music: NATIVITY   H. Lahee (d. 1912)

1. Come, let us join our cheerful songs
   With angels round the throne;
   Ten thousand thousand are their tongues,
   But all their joys are one.

2. 'Worthy the Lamb that died,' they cry,
   'To be exalted thus,'
   'Worthy the Lamb,' our lips reply,
   'For He was slain for us.'

3. Jesus is worthy to receive
   Honour and power divine;
   And blessings, more than we can give,
   Be, Lord, for ever Thine.

4. Let all that dwell above the sky,
   And air, and earth, and seas,
   Conspire to lift Thy glories high,
   And speak Thine endless praise.

5. The whole creation join in one
   To bless the sacred Name
   Of Him that sits upon the throne,
   And to adore the Lamb.

28. We are singing to You Lord

Words: M. V. Old

Music: STOWEY Mel. coll. C. J. Sharp (1859–1924)
Har. & arr. R. Vaughan Williams (1872–1958)

1. We are singing to You, Lord, our thanks and our joy,
   That You love every girl and You love every boy.
   We worship You, Lord, for You made everything;
   Teach us more of Yourself, till we make You our King.

2. We are singing to You, Lord, our joy at Your birth;
   You left glory in Heav'n to share our life on earth.
   You brought us forgiveness and joy, so we sing;
   Teach us more of Yourself, till we make You our King.

3. We are singing our thanks that You took all the shame
   For our sin when You died – t'was for this that You came.
   To You, dear Lord Jesus, our praises we bring;
   Teach us more of Yourself, till we make You our King.

29. Wide, wide as the ocean

Wide, wide as the ocean,
 High as the heaven above;
Deep, deep as the deepest sea
Is my Saviour's love.

I, though so unworthy,
Still am a child of His care;
For His Word teaches me
That His love reaches me everywhere.

30. Yesterday, today, for ever!

Yesterday, today, for ever, Jesus is the same;
All may change, but Jesus never,
Glory to His Name! glory to His Name! glory to His Name!
All may change, but Jesus never,
Glory to His Name!

31. Jesu's love is very wonderful

Words: H. W. Rattle

Music: Traditional Arr. D. J. Crawshaw

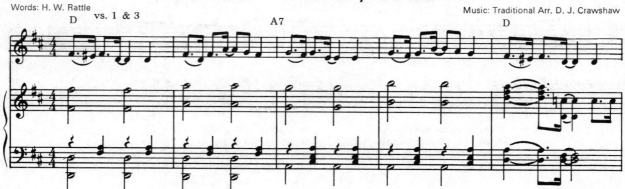

1. Jesu's love is very wonderful,
   Jesu's love is very wonderful,
   Jesu's love is very wonderful,
   Oh, wonderful love.

2. So high, can't get over it,
   So low, can't get under it,
   So wide, can't get round it,
   Oh, wonderful love.

3. Jesu's love is very wonderful,
   Jesu's love is very wonderful,
   Jesu's love is very wonderful,
   Oh, wonderful love.

32. At the name of Jesus

Words: C. M. Noel (d. 1877)

Music: CAMBERWELL   J. M. Brierley

1. At the name of Jesus
   Every knee shall bow,
   Every tongue confess Him
   King of glory now;
   'Tis the Father's pleasure
   We should call Him Lord,
   Who from the beginning
   Was the mighty Word.

2. At His voice creation
   Sprang at once to sight,
   All the angel faces,
   All the hosts of light;
   Thrones and dominations,
   Stars upon their way,
   All the heavenly orders
   In their great array.

3. Humbled for a season
   To receive a name
   From the lips of sinners,
   Unto whom He came;
   Faithfully He bore it
   Spotless to the last;
   Brought it back victorious
   When from death He passed.

4. Name Him, brothers, name Him
   With love strong as death,
   But with awe and wonder,
   And with bated breath;
   He is God the Saviour,
   He is Christ the Lord,
   Ever to be worshipped,
   Trusted and adored.

5. In your hearts enthrone Him;
   There let Him subdue
   All that is not holy,
   All that is not true;
   Crown Him as your Captain
   In temptation's hour,
   Let His will enfold you
   In its light and power.

6. Brothers, this Lord Jesus
   Shall return again,
   With His Father's glory,
   With His angel train;
   For all wreaths of empire
   Meet upon His brow,
   And our hearts confess Him
   King of glory now.

33. He's the same today

Words & Music: S. E. Cox

He's the same today as yesterday,
My great unchanging Friend;
He's the same today as yesterday,
Just the same unto the end.

By His mighty power He holds me,
In His arms of love enfolds me;
He's the same today as yesterday,
My great unchanging Friend.

34. Jesus is the Name we worship

Words: Diana Brand

Music: Alan Durden Arr. Alastair Durden

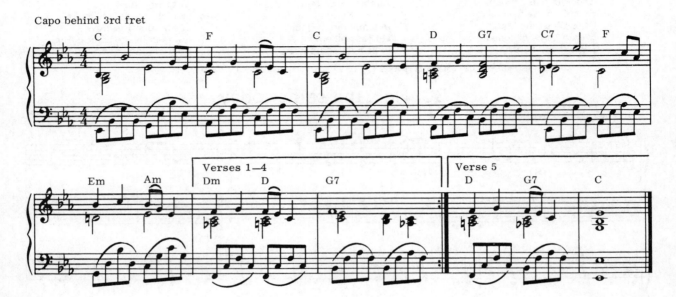

1. Jesus is the Name we worship,
   Jesus is the Friend we love,
   Jesus is our Lord and Saviour,
   King of heaven above.

2. Jesus knows when we are troubled,
   Jesus hears our every prayer,
   Jesus has our trials and sorrows
   Always in His care.

3. Jesus made the lame go walking,
   Jesus made the blind to see,
   Jesus healed the sick and wounded,
   Wondrous, O, was He.

4. Jesus is our great Redeemer,
   Jesus died for you and me,
   Jesus took our sins and failings,
   Bore them on the Tree.

5. Jesus lives within us daily,
   Jesus in our hearts will stay
   Till we meet with Him in Heaven
   On that glorious day.

35. There is no-one in the world like Jesus

Words: M. A. Baughen

Music: N. L. Warren

1. There is no-one in the world like Jesus,
   There is none that can compare with my Lord.
   Loving us, saving us,
   Knowing us, keeping us,
   Faithful Shepherd, gracious Friend.

   Chorus : There is no-one in the world like Jesus,
   There is none that can compare with my Lord.

2. If I go up to the heavens He is there.
   If I go down to the depths He's there too.
   Anywhere, everywhere,
   Anytime, all the time,
   He is with me evermore.
   Chorus :

3. Nothing in this world can ever separate
   The believer from the love of the Lord.
   Death or life, evil powers,
   Present things, coming things,
   None can part us from His love.
   Chorus :

36. Great was His kindness

Capo behind 1st fret

Music: F. Spencer Johnson

Great was His kindness, great was His love,
Sending my Saviour from Heaven above;
Marvellous kindness, marvellous love,
Reaching right down to me.

37. Sing His praises

Words: M. Cox

Sing His praises! Heaven raises
Songs to Him who died for me.
His the glory, mine the story
Of the love which sets me free;
Love which never will deceive me
Love which never lets me go.
Who can measure half the treasure
Of His love, who loves me so!

38. What a wonderful Saviour

Music: Arr. The Csehys

1. What a wonderful Saviour is Jesus,
   What a wonderful Friend is He,
   For He left all the glory of heaven,
   Came to earth to die on Calvary :

   Chorus : Sing Hosanna ! Sing Hosanna !
   Sing Hosanna to the King of kings !
   Sing Hosanna ! Sing Hosanna !
   Sing Hosanna to the King.

2. He arose from the grave, Hallelujah,
   And He lives never more to die,
   At the Father's right hand interceding
   He will hear and heed our faintest cry :
   Chorus :

3. He is coming some day to receive us,
   We'll be caught up to heaven above,
   What a joy it will be to behold Him,
   Sing forever of His grace and love.
   Chorus :

39. We will sing

Words G. Brattle & L. C. Barnes

Music: G. Brattle

We will sing of our Redeemer, He's our King:
All His glory, all His praise to you we bring:
With our hearts and with our voices Him we sing.
We love the Lord, we love His Word, He's our King.

40. Christ triumphant

Words: M. Şaward

Music: M. A. Baughen

Christ triumphant, ever reigning,
Saviour, Master, King—
Lord of heaven, our lives sustaining,
Hear us as we sing.
Yours the glory and the crown—
The high renown—
The eternal Name.

41. Let us praise

Words and music: G. Brattle

Let us praise, as we raise heart and voice to God above,
Let it ring, as we sing out the story of His love.
Let it flow, let it grow, let it rise from every shore:
Be adored, Christ the Lord, praise His Name for evermore!

42. Oh, thank the Lord

Words: Anon

Music: Traditional German air

Oh, thank the Lord, oh thank the Lord,
Give Him the praise for He is good;
Because His mercy does endure,
His faithfulness is ever sure;
Oh thank the Lord, oh thank the Lord,
Give Him the praise for He is good.

43. There's no greater Name

Words and music: M. A. Baughen

Capo behind 1st fret

There's no greater Name than Jesus.
Name of Him who came to save us,
In that saving Name of Jesus
Every knee should bow.
Let everything that is 'neath the ground,
Let everything in the world around,

Let everything that's high o'er the sky
Bow at Jesu's Name.
In our minds by faith professing,
In our hearts by inward blessing,
On our tongues by words confessing
Jesus Christ is Lord!

B. THE LORD JESUS CHRIST
1. When Jesus was born

44. O little town of Bethlehem

Words: P. Brooks (d.1893)

Music: FOREST GREEN English Traditional Melody
Coll. adpt. & arr. R. Vaughan Williams (d. 1958)

1. O little town of Bethlehem,
   How still we see thee lie !
   Above thy deep and dreamless sleep
   The silent stars go by ;
   Yet in thy dark streets shineth
   The everlasting Light ;
   The hopes and fears of all the years
   Are met in thee tonight.

2. O morning stars, together
   Proclaim the holy birth,
   And praises sing to God the King,
   And peace to men on earth ;
   For Christ is born of Mary,
   And gathered all above,
   While mortals sleep, the angels keep
   Their watch of wondering love.

3. How silently, how silently,
   The wondrous gift is given !
   So God imparts to human hearts
   The blessings of His heaven.
   No ear may hear His coming ;
   But in this world of sin,
   Where meek souls will receive Him, still
   The dear Christ enters in.

45. Infant holy

Words: Polish Carol Tr. E. M. G. Reed

Music: INFANT HOLY Polish Carol
Arr. A. E. Rusbridge

Capo behind 1st fret

1. Infant holy,
   Infant lowly.
   For His bed a cattle stall;
   Oxen lowing,
   Little knowing
   Christ the Babe is Lord of all.
   Swift are winging
   Angels singing,
   Nowells ringing,
   Tidings bringing,
   Christ the Babe is Lord of all.
   Christ the Babe is Lord of all.

2. Flocks were sleeping,
   Shepherds keeping
   Vigil till the morning new.
   Saw the glory,
   Heard the story,
   Tidings of a gospel true.
   Thus rejoicing,
   Free from sorrow,
   Praises voicing,
   Greet the morrow,
   Christ the Babe was born for you!
   Christ the Babe was born for you!

G–D

46. Advent song

Words and melody: Sister Oswin
Arr. D. J. Crawshaw

The world was in darkness
And nobody knew
The way to the Father
As you and I do.

They needed a light
That would show them the way;
And the great light shone
On Christmas Day.

47. Thou didst leave Thy throne

Words: E. E. S. Elliott (d. 1897)

Music: MARGARET   T. R. Matthews (d. 1910)

Capo behind 2nd fret

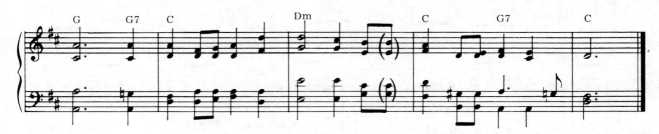

1. Thou didst leave Thy throne and Thy kingly crown,
When Thou camest to earth for me;
But in Bethlehem's home there was found no room
For Thy holy nativity.
O come to my heart, Lord Jesus!
There is room in my heart for Thee.

2. Heaven's arches rang when the angels sang,
Proclaiming Thy royal degree;
But of lowly birth cam'st Thou, Lord, on earth,
And in great humility.
O come to my heart, Lord Jesus!
There is room in my heart for Thee.

3. The foxes found rest, and the birds their nest
In the shade of the cedar tree;
But Thy couch was the sod, O Thou Son of God,
In the deserts of Galilee.
O come to my heart, Lord Jesus!
There is room in my heart for Thee.

4. Thou camest, O Lord, with the living word
That should set Thy children free;
But with mocking scorn, and with crown of thorn,
They bore Thee to Calvary.
O come to my heart, Lord Jesus!
Thy cross is my only plea.

5. When heaven's arches ring, and her choirs shall sing,
At Thy coming to victory,
Let Thy voice call me home, saying 'Yet there is room,
There is room at my side for thee.'
And my heart shall rejoice, Lord Jesus,
When Thou comest and callest for me.

48. No room

Words and music: H. M. Day

1. No room for the Baby at Bethlehem's inn,
   Only a cattle shed.
   No home on this earth for the dear Son of God,
   Nowhere to lay His head,
   Only a cross did they give to our Lord,
   Only a borrowed tomb.
   To-day He is seeking a place in your heart,
   Will you still say to Him 'No room'?

2. O Lord, in my heart there's a welcome for Thee.
   Gladly I now would say,
   Come in, blessed Saviour, my heart and my life
   Henceforth would own Thy sway.
   Long hast Thou waited and long knocked in vain
   Outside my heart's closed door;
   Oh, cleanse me from sin, then, dear Lord, enter in
   And dwell there for evermore.

49. Away in a manger

Words: Anon

Music: CRADLE SONG   W. J. Kirkpatrick (d. 1921)

1. Away in a manger, no crib for a bed,
   The little Lord Jesus laid down His sweet head.
   The stars in the bright sky looked down where He lay,
   The little Lord Jesus asleep in the hay.

2. The cattle are lowing, the Baby awakes,
   But little Lord Jesus, no crying He makes.
   I love You Lord Jesus! Look down from the sky,
   And stay by my side until morning is nigh.

3. Be near me, Lord Jesus; I ask You to stay
   Close by me for ever and love me, I pray.
   Bless all the dear children in Your tender care,
   And fit us for heaven to live with You there.

50. Once in royal David's city

Words: C. F. Alexander (d. 1895)

Music: IRBY   H. J. Gauntlett (d. 1876)

1. Once in royal David's city,
Stood a lowly cattle shed,
Where a mother laid her Baby
In a manger for His bed.
Mary was that mother mild,
Jesus Christ her little child.

2. He came down to earth from heaven,
Who is God and Lord of all,
And His shelter was a stable,
And His cradle was a stall:
With the poor and mean and lowly
Lived on earth our Saviour holy.

3. And through all His wondrous childhood
He would honour and obey,
Love and watch the lowly mother,
In whose gentle arms He lay.
Christian children all must be
Mild, obedient, good as He.

4. For He is our childhood's pattern:
Day by day like us He grew;
He was little, weak and helpless;
Tears and smiles like us He knew:
And He feeleth for our sadness,
And He shareth in our gladness.

5. And our eyes at last shall see Him,
Through His own redeeming love;
For that Child, so dear and gentle,
Is our Lord in heaven above;
And He leads His children on
To the place where He is gone.

6. Not in that poor, lowly stable,
With the oxen standing by,
We shall see Him—but in heaven,
Set at God's right hand on high;
When like stars His children crowned,
All in white shall wait around.

51. Jesus from glory

Words: J. E. Seddon

Music: M. A. Baughen & D. G. Wilson

Capo behind 4th fret

1. Jesus from glory to Bethlehem came,
   Born in a small wayside inn;
   He who created the worlds by His pow'r
   In grace came to save us from sin.

2. Jesus the Word to His own people came,
   Their true Redeemer and King;
   Him they rejected, His truth they despised,
   They spurned all the gifts He would bring.

3. Jesus the Saviour to Calvary came,
   Victim of hatred and strife;
   Flogged and disowned He was nailed to a cross,
   And yet by that death we have life.

4. Jesus the Lord out of death's bondage came,
   Victor o'er Satan and sin,
   Now in His pow'r He will dwell in our lives,
   And help us our victory to win.

5. Jesus the Master to your life will come,
   Bringing salvation and peace;
   In His glad service you'll find your reward
   And pleasures that never shall cease.

6. Jesus the Sovereign in glory shall come,
   Man's full redemption to bring;
   Saints of all ages their Lord shall acclaim,
   Their Saviour, their God and their King.

52. Christmas greetings

Words: C. M. Idle

Music: E. M. Stephenson Arr. Alastair Durden

1. Christmas greetings, Christmas joy
   For the new-born baby Boy!
   And for Jesus now we sing,
   Born a baby, born a King.

2. Born to laugh and born to cry,
   Born to live and born to die;
   Born to rise up from the grave,
   Born for sinners, born to save.

3. When the proper time had come
   God gave us His only Son;
   For the new-born baby Boy
   Christmas greetings, Christmas joy!

53. O ye joyful people

Words: Translated from the German by R. Heller   Music: O SANCTISSIMA   Arr. R. Heller

Optional Descant

O ye joyful ones, O ye happy ones,
Hallelujah! hallelujah!
Hallelujah! hallelujah!
Hallelujah! hallelujah, gloria!

1. O ye joyful people, O ye happy people,
Join the song that the angels sing.
Tidings of great joy they bring:
'Lo! this day is born a King.'
Hallelujah, hallelujah, Christ is born!

2. Praise God, all ye people, praise God, all mankind,
Sing, rejoice for our Christ has come.
Hark the heavenly host proclaim:
'Peace, good will on earth shall reign.'
Hallelujah, hallelujah, Christ is born!

3. Praise God, all ye people, praise God, all mankind.
Join the throng, at His manger kneel.
Unto us God sends His Son;
May His will on earth be done.
Hallelujah, hallelujah, Christ is born!

from 'Carols of the Nations' comp. Ruth Heller. Blandford Press Ltd.
originally published in 'Christmas Customs, Carols & Legends' by Schmitt, Hall and McCreary Company, U.S.A.

54. Angels from the realms of glory

Words: J. Montgomery (d. 1854)

Music: French Carol Melody Arr. Alastair Durden

1. Angels from the realms of glory,
   Wing your flight o'er all the earth;
   You who sang creation's story
   Now proclaim Messiah's birth:
   Chorus:
   Come and worship!
   Christ the new-born King.
   Come and worship!
   Worship Christ, the new-born King.

2. Shepherds in the fields abiding,
   Watching o'er your flocks by night;
   God with man is now residing,
   Yonder shines the Infant light:
   Chorus:

3. Sages, leave your contemplations,
   Brighter visions beam afar!
   Seek the great 'Desire of nations'.
   You have seen His natal star:
   Chorus:

55. When Jesus came from Heaven

Words: M. V. Old

Music: Old French Carol

1. When Jesus came from Heaven,
   The angels sang His birth;
   But little was the welcome
   We gave to Him on earth.
   The inn was closed against Him,
   'No room', they cried—and He,
   When Herod sought to kill Him,
   Became a refugee.

2. He came for love of you and
   He came for love of me;
   To take our sin upon Him
   And die at Calvary.
   That we might know forgiveness,
   His righteousness He gave,
   Come, see the Man of Sorrows,
   Who came to seek and save.

3. See—there He goes, the Saviour,
   A crown of thorns He wears.
   His back is sore and bleeding,
   And rough the cross He bears.
   Yet heavier far the sin that
   He carries there for me,
   'Tis love and grace that leads Him
   To pay my penalty.

56. The first Nowell

Words: Traditional

Music: THE FIRST NOWELL Traditional

Chorus

1. The first Nowell the angel did say
   Was to certain poor shepherds in fields as they lay;
   In fields where they lay keeping their sheep,
   On a cold winter's night that was so deep.
   Chorus: Nowell, Nowell, Nowell, Nowell,
   　　　　　Born is the King of Israel.

2. They lookèd up and saw a star
   Shining in the east, beyond them far,
   And to the earth it gave great light,
   And so it continued both day and night.
   Chorus:

3. And by the light of that same star,
   Three wise men came from country far;
   To seek for a King was their intent,
   And to follow the star wherever it went.
   Chorus:

4. This star drew nigh to the north-west;
   O'er Bethlehem it took its rest,
   And there it did both stop and stay
   Right over the place where Jesus lay.
   Chorus:

5. Then entered in those wise men three
   Full reverently upon their knee,
   And offered there in His presence
   Their gold, and myrrh, and frankincense.
   Chorus:

6. Then let us all with one accord
   Sing praises to our heavenly Lord,
   That hath made heaven and earth of nought,
   And with His blood mankind hath bought.
   Chorus:

57. While shepherds watched

Words: N. Tate (d. 1715)

Music: WINCHESTER OLD Este's Psalter 1592
© Cambridge University Press

1. While shepherds watched their flocks by night,
   All seated on the ground,
   The angel of the Lord came down,
   And glory shone around.

2. 'Fear not,' said he, for mighty dread
   Had seized their troubled mind;
   'Glad tidings of great joy I bring
   To you and all mankind.

3. 'To you in David's town, this day,
   Is born of David's line
   A Saviour, Who is Christ the Lord;
   And this shall be the sign.

4. 'The heavenly Babe you there shall find
   To human view displayed,
   All meanly wrapped in swathing bands,
   And in a manger laid.'

5. Thus spake the seraph; and forthwith
   Appeared a shining throng
   Of angels, praising God, who thus
   Addressed their joyful song:

6. 'All glory be to God on high,
   And on the earth be peace;
   Good-will henceforth from heaven to men
   Begin and never cease.'

58. The Virgin Mary had a baby boy

Melody from the Edric Connor Collection Arr. D. J. Crawshaw

1. The Virgin Mary had a baby boy,
   The Virgin Mary had a baby boy,
   The Virgin Mary had a baby boy,
   And they say that His name was Jesus.

Chorus: He come from the glory
         He come from the glorious kingdom;
         He come from the glory
         He come from the glorious kingdom;
         Oh, yes! believer.
         Oh, yes! believer.
         He come from the glory
         He come from the glorious kingdom.

2. The angels sang when the baby was born,
   The angels sang when the baby was born,
   The angels sang when the baby was born,
   And proclaimed Him the Saviour Jesus.
   Chorus:

3. The wise men saw where the baby was born,
   The wise men saw where the baby was born,
   The wise men saw where the baby was born,
   And they saw that His name was Jesus.
   Chorus:

59. Silent night

Words: J. Mohr (d. 1848) Tr. S. A. Brooke (d. 1916)   Music: STILLE NACHT F. Gruber (d. 1863)

Capo behind 1st fret

1. Silent night, holy night!
   Sleeps the world; hid from sight,
   Mary and Joseph in stable bare
   Watch o'er the Child beloved and fair
   Sleeping in heavenly rest,
   Sleeping in heavenly rest.

2. Silent night, holy night!
   Shepherds first saw the light;
   Heard resounding clear and long,
   Far and near, the angel song:
   'Christ the Redeemer is here',
   'Christ the Redeemer is here'.

3. Silent night, holy night!
   Son of God, O how bright
   Love is smiling from Thy face!
   Strikes for us now the hour of grace,
   Saviour, since Thou art born,
   Saviour, since Thou art born.

60. Calypso carol

Words and Music: Michael Perry Arr. Stephen Coates

1. See Him a-lying on a bed of straw;
   A draughty stable with an open door;
   Mary cradling the Babe she bore;
   The Prince of Glory is His name.
   Chorus: O now carry me to Bethlehem
   　　　　To see the Lord appear to men:
   　　　　Just as poor as was the stable then,
   　　　　The Prince of Glory when He came.

2. Star of silver sweep across the skies,
   Show where Jesus in the manger lies,
   Shepherds swiftly from your stupor rise
   To see the Saviour of the world.
   Chorus:

3. Angels, sing again the song you sang,
   Bring God's glory to the heart of man:
   Sing that Bethlehem's little Baby can
   Be salvation to the soul.
   Chorus:

4. Mine are riches—from Thy poverty:
   From Thine innocence, eternity;
   Mine, forgiveness by Thy death for me,
   Child of sorrow for my joy.
   Chorus:

61. O come, all ye faithful

Words: Tr. F. Oakeley (d. 1880) and others

Music: ADESTE FIDELES   18th Century Melody

1. O come, all ye faithful;
   Joyful and triumphant,
   O come ye, O come ye to Bethlehem;
   Come and behold Him,
   Born the King of angels:
   Chorus: O come, let us adore Him,
            O come, let us adore Him,
            O come, let us adore Him,
            Christ, the Lord.

2. God of God,
   Light of Light,
   Lo, He abhors not the Virgin's womb;
   Very God,
   Begotten, not created;
   Chorus:

3. Sing, choirs of angels,
   Sing in exultation,
   Sing, all ye citizens of heaven above;
   Glory to God
   In the highest:
   Chorus:

4. Yea, Lord, we greet Thee,
   Born this happy morning,
   Jesus, to Thee be glory given;
   Word of the Father,
   Now in flesh appearing:
   Chorus:

62. Emmanuel

Words and music: E. H. Swinstead (d. 1976)

Emmanuel, Emmanuel,
God who came on earth to dwell.
Who can all the story tell?
God with us, God with us,
God with us, Emmanuel.

63. Unto us a Boy is born

Words: German (15th Century)
Tr. Percy Dearmer (d. 1936)

Music: PUER NATUS
(German Carol Melody)
Harm. Martin Shaw (d. 1958)

1. Unto us a Boy is born!
   King of all creation,
   Came He to a world forlorn,
   The Lord of every nation.

2. Cradled in a stall was He
   With sleepy cows and asses;
   But the very beasts could see
   That He all men surpasses.

3. Herod then with fear was filled :
'A prince,' he said, 'in Jewry !'
All the little boys he killed
At Bethlehem in his fury.

4. Now may Mary's Son, who came
So long ago to love us,
Lead us all with hearts aflame
Unto the joys above us.

5. Alpha and Omega He !
Let the organ thunder,
While the choir with peals of glee
Doth rend the air asunder !

From 'The Oxford Book of Carols'. By permission of Oxford University Press

64. We three kings

Words and Music: J. H. Hopkins, Jnr. (d. 1891)

1. We three kings of Orient are ;
   Bearing gifts we traverse afar,
   Field and fountain, moor and mountain,
   Following yonder star :
   Chorus :   O star of wonder, star of night,
   Star with royal beauty bright,
   Westward leading, still proceeding,
   Guide us to thy perfect light.

2. Born a King on Bethlehem plain,
   Gold I bring, to crown Him again—
   King for ever, ceasing never,
   Over us all to reign :
   Chorus :

3. Frankincense to offer have I ;
   Incense owns a Deity nigh ;
   Prayer and praising all men raising,
   Worship Him, God most high :
   Chorus :

4. Myrrh is mine ; its bitter perfume
   Breathes a life of gathering gloom ;
   Sorrowing, sighing, bleeding, dying,
   Sealed in the stone-cold tomb :
   Chorus :

5. Glorious now, behold Him arise,
   King, and God, and sacrifice !
   Heaven sings 'Alleluia',
   'Alleluia' the earth replies :
   Chorus :

B. JESUS CHRIST
2. When Jesus lived on earth

65. Tell me the stories of Jesus

Words: W. H. Parker (d. 1929)　　　　Music: STORIES OF JESUS F. A. Challinor (d. 1952)

1. Tell me the stories of Jesus
   I love to hear;
   Things I would ask Him to tell me
   If He were here;
   Scenes by the wayside,
   Tales of the sea;
   Stories of Jesus,
   Tell them to me.

2. First let me hear how the children
   Stood round His knee;
   And I shall fancy His blessing
   Resting on me;
   Words full of kindness,
   Deeds full of grace,
   All in the lovelight
   Of Jesus' face.

3. Into the city I'd follow
   The children's band,
   Waving a branch of the palm tree
   High in my hand;
   One of His heralds,
   Yes, I would sing
   Loudest hosannas!
   Jesus is King!

4. Tell me, in accents of wonder,
   How rolled the sea,
   Tossing the boat in a tempest
   On Galilee!
   And how the Master,
   Ready and kind,
   Chided the billows,
   And hushed the wind.

5. Show me that scene in the garden
   Of bitter pain;
   Show me the cross where my Saviour
   For me was slain.
   Sad ones or bright ones,
   So that they be
   Stories of Jesus,
   Tell them to me.

6. Gladly I'd hear of His rising
   Out of the grave,
   Living and strong and triumphant,
   Mighty to save:
   And how He sends us
   All men to bring
   Stories of Jesus,
   Jesus, their King.

66. O the dark waves were raging

Words: W. H. Hamilton (d. 1958)

Music: STOWEY Melody coll.
C. Sharp (d. 1924)
Har. and arr. R. Vaughan
Williams (d. 1958)

Capo behind 1st fret

1. O the dark waves were raging, the boatmen in dread,
   But Jesus still slumbered, on pillow His head.
   No billows appalled Him with terror's alarm,
   For He knew underneath was His Father's strong arm.

2. But the boatmen in terror cried loud in their need:
   'Thy comrades' sore danger, Lord, dost Thou not heed?'
   Then Jesus awoke and arose with a will,
   Stretched His hands to the tempest and said 'Peace, be still'.

3. Then hushed were the billows and calm grew the night,
   All the storm sank to silence, and fled was their fright.
   We know that with Jesus the Lord at our side
   No danger shall daunt us, whatever betide.

Words: from 'Children Praising', music from 'Enlarged Songs of Praise'. By permission of Oxford University Press

67. A Man once came from Galilee

Words: M. V. Old

Music: TYROLESE

1. A Man once came from Galilee,
   No Man so great as He.
   We left our work and went with Him,
   His followers to be.
       Lord Jesus, be our Teacher now,
       And may we learn from You
       To love and serve the Father God
       And other people, too.

2. We saw our Master heal the sick;
   We saw His love for men.
   We saw His power reach out to touch
   And bring to life again.
       Lord Jesus, be our Healer now,
       And make us whole and strong
       That we may share Your love and power
       And serve You all day long.

3. They nailed Him to a cross of wood;
   They scoffed and watched Him die.
   And we could not at first believe
   That He would reign on high.
       Lord Jesus, be our Saviour now,
       And may we all repent
       And hate the sin that brought You down
       To bear our punishment.

4. We saw the stone was rolled away
   Before the empty grave.
   We met the risen Lord of life,
   The one who came to save.
       Lord Jesus, You are God and King;
       Oh, may we all obey
       And glorify You, risen Lord,
       In all we do each day.

(The first half of each verse can be sung by a small group representing the disciples, everyone else then singing the second half of each verse.)

68. Let's talk about Jesus

Words and music: H. Buffum, Jr.

Capo behind 1st fret

Let's talk about Jesus, the King of kings is He,
The Lord of lords supreme, thro' all eternity
The Great I AM, the Way, the Truth, the Life, the Door.
Let's talk about Jesus more and more.

69. I am the Way, the Truth and the Life

Music: Traditional Arr. D. J. Crawshaw

I am the Way, the Truth and the Life,
That's what Jesus said.
I am the Way, the Truth and the Life,
That's what Jesus said.
Without the Way there is no going,
Without the Truth there is no knowing,
Without the Life there is no living,
I am the Way, the Truth and the Life,
That's what Jesus said.

70. It was a miracle

Words and music: Betty Lou Mills

1. When Jesus heard that His very good friend
        call'd Lazarus had died,
   He went to the grave and cried real tears,
   Then He told him to come alive.
   It was a miracle,
   It was a miracle,
   It was a miracle and it's true.
   It was a miracle,
   It was a miracle,
   'Cause that's what Jesus did do.

2. So they took the bandages off him and he stood up
        strong and straight.
   Then the people around all 'oohed' and 'ahed'
   As he sat right down and ate.
   It was a miracle,
   It was a miracle,
   It was a miracle and it's true.
   It was a miracle,
   It was a miracle,
   'Cause that's what Jesus did do.

71. By blue Galilee

Words and music: E. H. Swinstead (d. 1976)

By blue Galilee Jesus walked of old,
By blue Galilee wondrous things He told.
Saviour, still my Teacher be,
Showing wondrous things to me,
As of old by Galilee, blue Galilee.

72. Amen

Words and melody: Negro Spiritual Arr. Alan Durden

1. See the baby,
   Lying in a manger,
   One Christmas morning;

Chorus: Amen, Amen, Amen, Amen, Amen.

2. See Him in the temple,
   Talking to the Elders,
   How they marvelled at His wisdom;

3. See Him at the seaside,
   Preaching and healing
   To the blind and feeble;

4. See Him in the garden,
   Praying to His Father,
   In deepest sorrow;

5. Yes, He is my Saviour,
   Jesus died to save us,
   And rose on Easter;

6. Hallelujah!
   In the Kingdom
   With my Saviour;

It is suggested that the chorus is
sung through once before Verse 1.

73. Only Jesus

Words and music: Betty Lou Mills

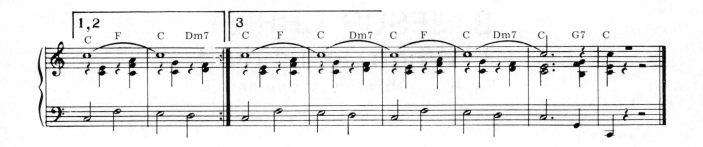

1. Who took fish and bread, hungry people fed?
   Who changed water into wine?
   Who made well the sick, who made see the blind?
   Who touched earth with feet divine?
   Only Jesus, only Jesus, only He has done this:
   Who made live the dead? Truth and kindness spread?
   Only Jesus did all this.

2. Who walked dusty road? Cared for young and old?
   Who sat children on His knee?
   Who spoke words so wise? Filled men with surprise?
   Who gave all, but charged no fee?
   Only Jesus, only Jesus, only He has done this:
   Who in death and grief spoke peace to a thief?
   Only Jesus did all this.

3. Who soared through the air? Joined His Father there?
   He has you and me in view:
   He, who this has done, is God's only Son,
   And He's int'rested in you.
   Only Jesus, only Jesus, only He has done this:
   He can change a heart, give a new fresh start,
   Only He can do this.

B. JESUS CHRIST
3. When Jesus died
74. It is a thing most wonderful

Words W. W. How (d. 1897)

Music: GIDEON T. B. Southgate (d. 1868)

1st tune GIDEON

1. It is a thing most wonderful,
   Almost too wonderful to be,
   That God's own Son should come from heaven
   And die to save a child like me.

2. And yet I know that it is true;
   He came to this poor world below,
   And wept and toiled and mourned and died,
   Only because He loved us so.

3. I cannot tell how He could love
   A child so weak and full of sin;
   His love must be most wonderful,
   If He could die my love to win.

4. I sometimes think about His cross
   And shut my eyes, and try to see
   The cruel nails, and crown of thorns,
   And Jesus crucified for me.

5. But even could I see Him die,
   I could but see a little part
   Of that great love which, like a fire,
   Is always burning in His heart.

6. It is most wonderful to know
   His love for me so free and sure;
   But 'tis more wonderful to see
   My love for Him so faint and poor.

7. And yet I want to love Thee, Lord:
   O light the flame within my heart,
   And I will love Thee more and more
   Until I see Thee as Thou art!

Music: HERONGATE English Traditional Melody. Coll., arr. and harm.
R. Vaughan Williams (1872–1958)

2nd tune HERONGATE

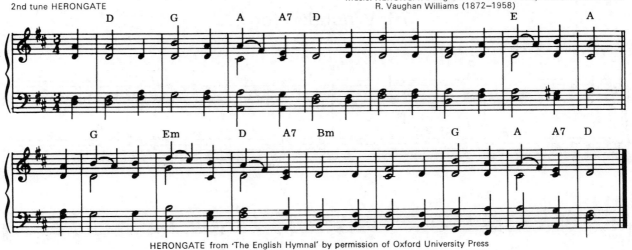

75. Higher than the hills

Words and music: N. J. Clayton

Higher than the hills,
Deeper than the sea,
Broader than the skies above
Is my Redeemer's love for me;

To His cross of shame
Jesus freely came,
Bearing all my sin and sorrow,
Wondrous love !

76. Wounded for me!

Words and music: W. G. Ovens

Capo behind 1st fret

Wounded for me! Wounded for me!
There on the cross He was wounded for me:
Gone my transgressions, and now I am free,
All because Jesus was wounded for me.

77. There is a green hill

Words C. F. Alexander (d. 1895)

Music: HORSLEY W. Horsley (d. 1858)

1st tune HORSLEY
Capo behind 3rd fret

2nd tune THE HOUSE OF THE RISING SUN   Traditional Arr. A. Price

1. There is a green hill far away,
   Outside a city wall,
   Where the dear Lord was crucified,
   Who died to save us all.

2. We may not know, we cannot tell,
   What pains He had to bear;
   But we believe it was for us
   He hung and suffered there.

3. He died that we might be forgiven,
   He died to make us good,
   That we might go at last to heaven
   Saved by His precious blood.

4. There was no other good enough
   To pay the price of sin;
   He only could unlock the gate
   Of heaven, and let us in.

5. O dearly, dearly has He loved!
   And we must love Him too,
   And trust in His redeeming blood,
   And try His works to do.

78. Jesus loved us

Words: M. V. Old

Music: Traditional Arr. D. Parsons

Jesus loved us, and He died for us,
That from sin we might be
Saved by Him, who wants to give to us
Life eternal and free.
Then we shall—
Thank Him for His grace that leads us to believe,
Praise Him that His Spirit we can now receive,
Give Him love's obedience, as to Him we turn,
Live for Him, and from Him learn.

79. He did not come to judge

He did not come to judge the world,
He did not come to blame;
He did not only come to seek,
It was to save He came;

And when we call Him Saviour,
And when we call Him Saviour,
And when we call Him Saviour,
Then we call Him by His name.

80. On Calvary's tree

Words: A. W. Edsor

Music: Melody A. E. Walton from 'Call of the Angelus'
Adapted by A. W. Edsor

Capo behind 4th fret

On Calvary's tree He died for me,
That I His love might know.
To set me free He died for me,
That's why I love Him so.

© Melody—Lafleur & Son Ltd.
© Words—Kingsway Publications Ltd.

81. Jesus died to set me free

Words: G. R. Furlong

Music A. F. Mordaunt Smith

Jesus died to set me free
From the guilt of sin;
Jesus lives that I may be
Strong the fight to win.

82. He laid down His life

Words and music: E. P. Graham

He laid down His life for His sheep,
He laid down His life for His sheep.
This Shepherd so kind had me in His mind,
When He laid down His life for His sheep.

83. Jesus died for all the children

Capo behind 1st fret

Jesus died for all the children,
All the children of the world.
Red and yellow, black and white,
All are precious in His sight:
Jesus died for all the children of the world.

84. For God so loved the world

Words: F. Townsend

Music: A. B. Smith

For God so loved the world,
He gave His only Son
To die on Calvary's tree,
From sin to set me free;
Some day He's coming back,
What glory that will be,
Wonderful His love to me.

85. What do I see

Words and music: F. Parsonage

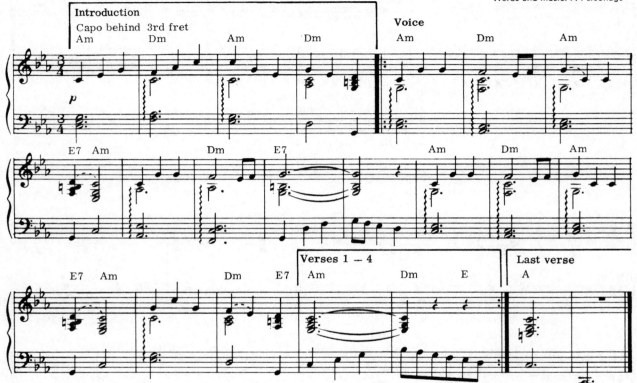

1. What do I see as I gaze down the road?
   People are waiting to jeer;
   I see a man who is bearing His load,
   Wood of the Cross that men fear.

2. Only a short time ago, these people
   Greeted this man as a King,
   Waving palm branches and shouting hosanna,
   Making the countryside ring.

3. He had brought healing, and often had spoken
   Good news that God sets us free,
   In His disciples new hope was awoken,
   Faith hope and charity.

4. What do I see as I gaze down the road?
   People still jeering ahead;
   I see a man who is nailed to His Cross,
   Jesus the victim is dead.

5. What do I see as I look up in prayer?
   What makes my heart want to sing?
   I see a man who is living for ever,
   Jesus the Saviour is King.

B. JESUS CHRIST
4. When Jesus came alive again
86. Jesus Christ is risen today

Words: Lyra Davidica (1708)

Music: LLANFAIR Melody R. Williams (d. 1821)

1. Jesus Christ is risen today, Hallelujah!
   Our triumphant holy day, Hallelujah!
   Who did once, upon the cross, Hallelujah!
   Suffer to redeem our loss. Hallelujah!

2. Hymns of praise then let us sing, Hallelujah!
   Unto Christ, our heavenly King, Hallelujah!
   Who endured the cross and grave, Hallelujah!
   Sinners to redeem and save. Hallelujah!

3. But the pains which He endured, Hallelujah!
   Our salvation have procured, Hallelujah!
   Now in heaven above He's King, Hallelujah!
   Where the angels ever sing Hallelujah!

87. Sing and rejoice

To be sung as a round, unaccompanied

Sing and rejoice,
Sing and rejoice.
Jesus has risen,
Come, lift up your voice.

88. The angel rolled the stone away

Words: P. O. Smith

Music: Negro Spiritual Arr. D. J. Crawshaw

Chorus : The angel rolled the stone away,
The angel rolled the stone away.
It was early Easter Sunday morning,
The angel rolled the stone away.

1. Mary came a-running about the break of day,
   Looking for Lord Jesus ; the stone was rolled away.
   Chorus :

2. She sadly walked the garden, a shadow barred her way ;
   'Please tell me, Mr. Gardener, who rolled the stone away ?'
   Chorus :

3. She waited for an answer, 'Mary' He did say.
   'Rabboni ! Oh my Master, You have rolled the stone away.'
   Chorus :

4. He's returned, from darkness, and He's here to stay ;
   Fear no more, my brothers—angels rolled the stone away.
   Chorus :

89. I cannot tell

Words and music: E. H. Swinstead (d. 1976)

I cannot tell how Christ my Lord should rise
Out from the grave that glorious Easter-tide ;
Or rising, pass triumphant through the skies,
To God's right hand in heaven glorified ;
But this I know, His death was not the end,
That now He lives, He lives to be my Friend.

90. Low in the grave He lay

Words and music: CHRIST AROSE R. Lowry (d. 1899)

1. Low in the grave He lay,
   Jesus, my Saviour !
   Waiting the coming day,
   Jesus, my Lord !

   Chorus : Up from the grave He arose
             With mighty triumph o'er His foes;
             He arose a Victor from the dark domain,
             And He lives for ever with His saints to reign !
             He arose ! He arose ! Hallelujah ! Christ arose !

2. Vainly they watch His bed,
   Jesus, my Saviour !
   Vainly they seal the dead,
   Jesus, my Lord !
   Chorus :

3. Death cannot keep his prey,
   Jesus, my Saviour !
   He tore the bars away,
   Jesus, my Lord !
   Chorus :

91. Jesus Christ is risen, Alleluia

Words and music: F. Parsonage

1. Jesus Christ is risen, Alleluia,
   What a wonderful happy day!
   Jesus lives for ever, Alleluia,
   Christians everywhere join with us and say:

2. Jesus Christ the Saviour, Alleluia,
   Has this day the victory won.
   He has conquered death, Alleluia,
   One and all sing praises to the Son.

3. Tell the whole wide world, Alleluia,
   Send the message far on its way.
   Jesus Christ is risen, Alleluia,
   Christians celebrate this great Easter day.

4. Alleluia, Alleluia,
   Alleluia to our Lord.
   Let the world sing Alleluia,
   Alleluia to the Son our Lord.

92. He lives

Words and music: A. H. Ackley

Capo behind 1st fret

He lives ! He lives !
Christ Jesus lives today !
He walks with me and talks with me
Along life's narrow way.

He lives ! He lives,
Salvation to impart !
You ask me how I know He lives—
He lives within my heart !

93. Be glad and sing

Words and music: D. L. Braun

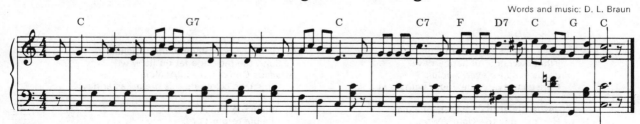

Be glad and sing, for Jesus is alive ;
Be glad and sing, for Jesus is alive.
He died my soul to save,
He rose up from the grave ;
Be glad and sing for Jesus lives !

94. He rose triumphantly

Words: O. J. Smith

Music: B. D. Ackley

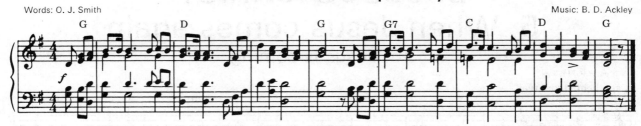

He rose triumphantly,
In pow'r and majesty,
The Saviour rose no more to die.
Oh, let us now proclaim
The glory of His Name,
And tell to all, He lives to-day.

95. The stone was rolled away

Music: E. H. G. Sargent (d. 1974)

The stone was rolled away
From where the Saviour lay,
That glad and glorious day
When Jesus rose again.

A living Saviour is He,
From sin to set me free;
To Him all glory be
Who died and rose again.

B. JESUS CHRIST
5. When Jesus comes again
96. Jesus is coming

Words: H. G. Phillipson

Music: C. Hazlehurst

Jesus is coming to earth once again,
Jesus is coming in glory to reign.
If we but love Him, how glorious a thing
To see Him and hear Him and serve Him as King.

97. When He comes

Words: T. Dudley-Smith
Music: J. D. Thornton

1. When He comes,
   When He comes,
   We shall see the Lord in glory when He comes,
   As I read the gospel story
   We shall see the Lord in glory,
   We shall see the Lord in glory when He comes.
      With the Alleluias ringing to the sky,
      With the Alleluias ringing to the sky,
      As I read the gospel story
      We shall see the Lord in glory
      With the Alleluias ringing to the sky !

2. When He comes,
   When He comes,
   We shall hear the trumpet sounded when He comes,
   We shall hear the trumpet sounded,
   See the Lord by saints surrounded,
   We shall hear the trumpet sounded when He comes !

With the Alleluias ringing to the sky,
With the Alleluias ringing to the sky,
We shall hear the trumpet sounded,
See the Lord by saints surrounded,
With the Alleluias ringing to the sky !

3. When He comes,
   When He comes,
   We shall all rise up to meet Him when He comes,
   When He calls His own to greet Him,
   We shall all rise up to meet Him,
   We shall all rise up to meet Him when He comes.
      With the Alleluias ringing to the sky,
      With the Alleluias ringing to the sky,
      When He calls His own to greet Him,
      We shall all rise up to meet Him,
      With the Alleluias ringing to the sky.

Repeat Verse 1.

98. Living, He loved me

Words: J. Wilbur Chapman (1854-1918)

Music: C. H. Marsh

Capo behind 1st fret

Living, He loved me; dying, He saved me;
Buried, He carried my sins far away;
Rising, He justified freely for ever;
One day He's coming—O glorious day!

C. THE HOLY SPIRIT
99. Holy Spirit, hear us

Words: W. H. Parker (d. 1929)

Music: ERNSTEIN   J. F. Swift (d. 1931)

1. Holy Spirit, hear us,
   Help us while we sing;
   Breathe into the music
   Of the praise we bring.

2. Holy Spirit, prompt us
   When we kneel to pray;
   Nearer come and teach us
   What we ought to say.

3. Holy Spirit, teach us
   When Thy Word we read;
   Shine upon its pages
   With the light we need.

4. Holy Spirit, give us
   Each a lowly mind;
   Make us more like Jesus,
   Gentle, pure and kind.

5. Holy Spirit, help us
   Daily by Thy might,
   What is wrong to conquer,
   And to choose the right.

100. A Samaritan on a lonely road

Words: M. V. Old

Music: WRAGGLE TAGGLE GYPSIES Traditional
arr. E. M. Stephenson

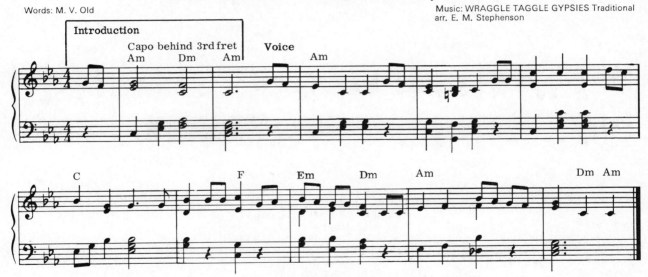

1. A Samaritan on a lonely road
   Wouldn't turn aside from a wounded man;
   He bound up his wounds, he gave money, he gave time.
   'Let me help,' said he, 'in any way I can'.

2. We can help at home, we can help at school
   And our help is needed where'er we go;
   For love of our Lord we can show to all we meet
   That the loving Lord is One they, too, can know.

3. But a greater Helper for Jesu's friends
   Is the Holy Spirit who helps us still
   To grow more like Christ, to be wise and true and good,
   And to know and do our Heavenly Father's will.

101. Holy Spirit came as fire

Words: E. M. Wyatt & B. J. Ogden

Music: Melody EVERY STAR SHALL SING A CAROL
S. Carter,   Arrangement Alan Durden

1. Holy Spirit came as fire,
   Followers of Christ to bless,
   So that full of might and power,
   They their Master did confess,
   Praised His name, preached the Word,
   Called men to accept the Lord.

2. Holy Spirit, power of Jesus,
   Make us strong to work and fight,
   So that when we meet with evil
   We may conquer in Your might.
   Through Your name, by Your Word,
   We are soldiers of the Lord.

102. Spirit of God, unseen as the wind

Words: M. V. Old

Music: SKYE BOAT SONG Traditional
arr. Alastair Durden

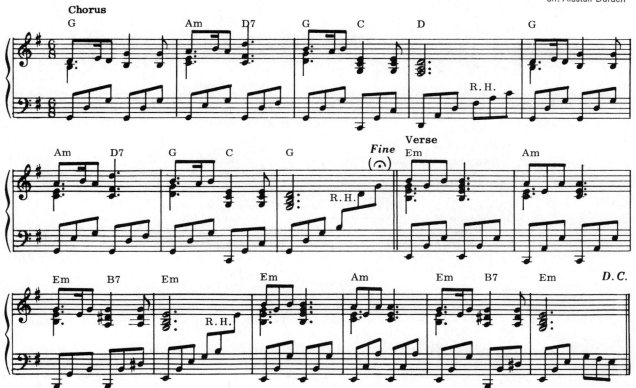

Chorus: Spirit of God, unseen as the wind,
Gentle as is the dove;
Teach us the truth and help us believe,
Show us the Saviour's love.

1. You spoke to men long, long ago,
Gave us the written Word;
We read it still, needing its truth,
Through it God's voice is heard.
Chorus:

2. Without Your help we fail our Lord,
We cannot live His way;
We need Your power, we need Your strength,
Following Christ each day.
Chorus:

103. When God the Holy Spirit

Words: M. E. Knollys

Music: MILDRED M. E. Knollys

1. When God the Holy Spirit
   Came down on Whitsunday,
   He taught the friends of Jesus
   Just what to do and say.

2. When God the Holy Spirit
   Speaks to my heart, I know
   He'll teach me and He'll help me
   And with me always go.

3. I will be still and listen
   And hear this gentle Friend,
   Who bids me look at Jesus
   And follow to the end.

4. I love the Holy Spirit,
   And to this Friend I'll pray:
   'O come, most Holy Spirit,
   Be with me every day.'

104. With the Father when the world began

Words: E. M. Stephenson

Music: MARIANINA   Traditional
arr. E. M. Stephenson

1. With the Father when the world began,
   Resting on the Christ, the Son of Man,
   Holy Spirit, bringing in God's plan,
   You are with us still today—
   Chorus: And You show us Jesu's way.
           Let us praise You now and say—
           Holy Spirit, Holy Spirit,
           Help us understand You and obey.

2. Just before they saw our Lord ascend
   Christ's disciples heard how He would send
   One who'd bring new life and be their Friend,
   And You're with us still today—
   Chorus:

3. Like a fire and wind You came to men
   When at Pentecost they prayed, and then,
   Preaching Christ, they showed God's power again.
   You are with us still today—
   Chorus:

4. Still You live within God's children here,
   Giving boldness and removing fear,
   Love, joy, peace and gentleness appear
   As we prove Your power today.
   Chorus:

D. WHAT GOD WANTS OF US
105. My Lord, my God, I know You see

Words: M. V. Old

Music: MA NORMANDIE   Arr. D. Parsons

1. My Lord, my God, I know You see
   The shameful things deep down in me;
   My thoughts, my words, the things I do
   That spoil my life—they strike at You.
   Lord God on high, You sent Your Son
   To die for sin—and I am one
   Whose sin drove Him to Calvary.
   Forgive me, Lord—I know He died for me.

2. My Lord, my God, please make me see
   How grieved You are because of me,
   And help me to own up to You
   About the things I've failed to do.
   Lord God on high, You sent Your Son
   To die for sin—and I am one
   Whose sin drove Him to Calvary.
   Forgive me, Lord—I know He died for me.

3. Lord Jesus Christ, from sin I turn,
   Please take my life and make it new.
   Give me Your goodness; let me learn
   To show my trust by serving You.
   Lord Jesus Christ, Your Spirit send
   To live in me, and be my Friend.
   I will obey You, Saviour-King.
   I love You, Lord—Your praises I will sing.

106. Jesus is knocking

Words and music: G. Brattle

Jesus is knocking, patiently waiting,
Outside your heart's closed door.
Do not reject Him, simply accept Him,
Now and for evermore.

© G. Brattle

107. No other door

Words and music: H. T. Combe

No other door; no other way;
No other guide to the realms of day;
No other keeper when tempted to stray;
No other friend like Jesus.

108. O God of faith

Words: R. Hopgood

Music: Traditional Arr. D. J. Crawshaw

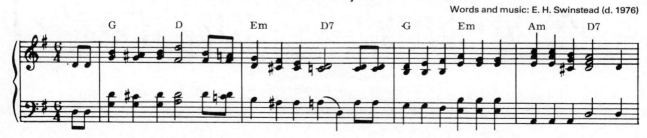

1. O God of faith, help me believe.
   Help me to know You shelter me,
   And tho' Your face I cannot see
   Oh may I feel Your strength in me.

2. O God of hope, help me to know
   That hope in You is strong and sure,
   That You raised Jesus from the grave,
   And hope is in Your power to save.

3. O God of love, help me to see
   That love sent Christ to die for me.
   And though unworthy I can say
   That love endures from day to day.

4. O God of faith, help me believe,
   O God of hope my Saviour be.
   O God of love show love through me,
   And shine for all the world to see.

109. There's a way back to God

Words and music: E. H. Swinstead (d. 1976)

There's a way back to God from the dark paths of sin;
There's a door that is open and you may go in;
At Calvary's cross is where you begin,
When you come as a sinner to Jesus.

110. Calvary

Words: N. Shaxson

Music: T. S. Shaxson

Out there amongst the hills
My Saviour died;
Pierced by those cruel nails,
Was crucified.
Lord Jesus, Thou hast done
All this for me;
Henceforward I would live
Only for Thee.

111. Somebody's knocking

Music: Traditional Arr. M. C. T. Strover

1. Somebody's knocking at your door,
Somebody's knocking at your door,
O sinner, why don't you answer?
Somebody's knocking at your door.

2. Knocks like Jesus,
Somebody's knocking at your door;
Knocks like Jesus,
Somebody's knocking at your door.
O sinner, why don't you answer?
Somebody's knocking at your door.

3. Can't you hear Him?
   Somebody's knocking at your door;
   Can't you hear Him?
   Somebody's knocking at your door.
   O sinner, why don't you answer?
   Somebody's knocking at your door.

4. Answer Jesus,
   Somebody's knocking at your door;
   Answer Jesus,
   Somebody's knocking at your door.
   O sinner, why don't you answer?
   Somebody's knocking at your door.

112. Cleanse me

Words and music: R. Hudson Pope (d. 1967)

Cleanse me from my sin, Lord,
Put Your pow'r within, Lord,
Take me as I am, Lord,
And make me all Your own.

Keep me day by day, Lord,
Underneath Your sway, Lord,
Make my heart Your palace,
And Your royal throne.

113. Into the hands

Capo behind 1st fret

Words and music: E. H. Swinstead (d. 1976)

Into the hands that were wounded to save me,
Into the hands that are mighty to keep,

Into the hands that can guide me and guard me,
Saviour, my life I yield.

114. O Jesus, I have promised

Words: J. E. Bode (d. 1874)

Music: DAY OF REST
J. W. Elliott (d. 1915)

1st tune

1. O Jesus, I have promised
   To serve Thee to the end;
   Be Thou for ever near me,
   My Master and my Friend;
   I shall not fear the battle
   If Thou art by my side,
   Nor wander from the pathway
   If Thou wilt be my Guide.

2. O let me feel Thee near me,
   The world is ever near;
   I see the sights that dazzle,
   The tempting sounds I hear;
   My foes are ever near me,
   Around me and within;
   But Jesus, draw Thou nearer,
   And shield my soul from sin.

3. O let me hear Thee speaking
   In accents clear and still,
   Above the storms of passion,
   The murmurs of self-will;
   O speak to reassure me,
   To hasten, or control;
   O speak, and make me listen,
   Thou Guardian of my soul.

4. O Jesus, Thou hast promised
   To all who follow Thee,
   That where Thou art in glory,
   There shall Thy servants be;
   And, Jesus, I have promised
   To serve Thee to the end:
   O give me grace to follow,
   My Master and my Friend.

5. O let me see Thy footmarks,
   And in them plant mine own;
   My hope to follow duly
   Is in Thy strength alone.
   O guide me, call me, draw me,
   Uphold me to the end;
   And then in heaven receive me,
   My Saviour and my Friend.

2nd tune

115. Come and serve the master

Words and music: M. G. Archibald

Come and serve the Master,
He alone is true:
He will pardon sinners,
Therefore pardon you . . .
He has promised power,
Power to all who ask,
Power to conquer Satan,
Power for every task.

116. Choose you this day

Music: E. H. Swinstead (d. 1976)

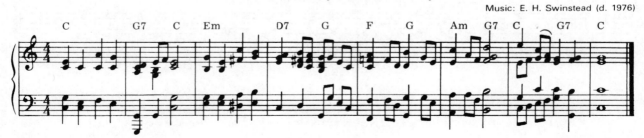

Choose you this day whom you will serve;
Choose you this day whom you will serve;
But as for me, as for me, as for me, as for me,
I will serve the Lord.

117. We want to tell you of Jesu's love

Words: M. V. Old

Music: ES BUUREBUEBLI Swiss Folk
Tune Arr. C. Simmonds

1. We want to tell you of Jesu's love,
    How He left His glory in Heav'n above
    And came, a Baby, to Bethlehem's stall,
    To show God's love for us all.
    Chorus: Follow Him! Follow Him! He has borne our sin,
    That we might be free and clean within.
    Turn then to Jesus and crown Him King,
    Your Lord in everything.

2. As Man He shared all our life on earth,
    To a shameful death from a lowly birth,
    As God He made all our sin His own,
    That He for us might atone.
    Chorus:

3. He died that we might forgiveness know,
    Share His Spirit's power in our life below;
    And then His glory in Heaven we'll share,
    And praise our Saviour there.
    Chorus:

118. All that I am, He made me

Words: H. R. Jones

Music: J. Ward

All that I am, He made me;
All that I have He gave me;
And all that ever I hope to be,
Jesus alone must do for me.

119. Follow, follow!

Music: R. Lowry

Capo behind 1st fret

Follow, follow, I would follow Jesus,
Anywhere, everywhere, I would follow on;
Follow, follow, I would follow Jesus,
Ev'rywhere He leads me, I would follow on.

120. Fisherman Peter

Music: South Carolina Spiritual

1. Fisherman Peter on the sea,
   Drop your net boy, and follow Me!
   Fisherman Peter on the sea,
   Drop your net boy, and follow Me!

2. Rich young ruler, plain to see,
   Can't love money and follow Me!   } twice

3. Lonely Zaccheus in the tree,
   Love your neighbour and follow Me!   } twice

4. Nicodemus Pharisee,
   New life comes when you follow Me!   } twice

5. Doubting Thomas, from doubt be free,
   Stop your doubting and follow Me!   } twice

E. LIVING AS GOD'S FRIENDS

121. Father, hear the prayer we offer

Words: L. M. Willis (d. 1908)

Music: SUSSEX from an English Traditional Melody
Coll., adpt. and harm.
R. Vaughan Williams (d. 1958)

1. Father, hear the prayer we offer!
   Not for ease that prayer shall be,
   But for strength that we may ever
   Live our lives courageously.

2. Not for ever in green pastures
   Do we ask our way to be:
   But by steep and rugged pathways
   Would we strive to climb to Thee.

3. Not for ever by still waters
   Would we idly quiet stay:
   But would smite the living fountains
   From the rocks along our way.

4. Be our strength in hours of weakness,
   In our wanderings be our Guide,
   Through endeavour, failure, danger,
   Father, be Thou at our side.

Music: From 'The English Hymnal' by permission of Oxford University Press

122. Lord of the loving heart

Music: N. Nettleton

Lord of the loving heart, may mine be loving too.
Lord of the gentle hands, may mine be gentle too.
Lord of the willing feet, may mine be willing too;
So may I grow more like Thee in all I say and do.

123. Like Jesus

Words: I. S. Taylor

Music: R. Hudson Pope (d. 1967)

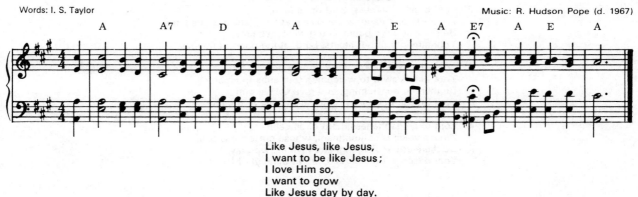

Like Jesus, like Jesus,
I want to be like Jesus;
I love Him so,
I want to grow
Like Jesus day by day.

124. Lord of all hopefulness

Words: Jan Struther (d. 1953)

Music: SLANE   Har. M. Shaw (1875–1958)

1. Lord of all hopefulness, Lord of all joy,
   Whose trust, ever child-like, no cares could destroy,
   Be there at our waking, and give us, we pray,
   Your bliss in our hearts, Lord, at the break of the day.

2. Lord of all eagerness, Lord of all faith,
   Whose strong hands were skilled at the plane and the lathe,
   Be there at our labours, and give us, we pray,
   Your strength in our hearts, Lord, at the noon of the day.

3. Lord of all kindliness, Lord of all grace,
   Your hands swift to welcome, Your arms to embrace,
   Be there at our homing, and give us, we pray,
   Your love in our hearts, Lord, at the eve of the day.

4. Lord of all gentleness, Lord of all calm,
   Whose voice is contentment, whose presence is balm,
   Be there at our sleeping, and give us, we pray,
   Your peace in our hearts, Lord, at the end of the day.

125. Evidence

Words and music: A. E. Rennix

Let it be seen that with Thee I have been,
Jesus, my Lord and my Saviour;
Let it be known I am truly Thine own,
By all my speech and behaviour.

126. Jesus supreme in my heart

Words and music: W. J. Graham Hobson

Jesus, supreme in my heart,
Bid ev'ry rival depart;
Teach me, I pray, with joy to obey,
Jesus supreme in my heart.

127. Heavenly Father, may Thy blessing

Words: W. Charter Piggott (d. 1943)

Music: PLEADING SAVIOUR   Plymouth
Collection (USA) 1855 harm.
R. Vaughan Williams (1872–1958)

1. Heavenly Father, may Thy blessing
   Rest upon Thy children now,
   When in praise Thy name they hallow,
   When in prayer to Thee they bow:
   In the wondrous story reading
   Of the Lord of truth and grace,
   May they see Thy love reflected
   In the light of His dear face.

2. May they learn from this great story
   All the arts of friendliness;
   Truthful speech and honest action,
   Courage, patience, steadfastness;
   How to master self and temper,
   How to make their conduct fair;
   When to speak and when be silent,
   When to do and when forbear.

3. May His Spirit wise and holy,
   With His gifts their spirits bless,
   Make them loving, joyous, peaceful,
   Rich in goodness, gentleness,
   Strong in self-control, and faithful,
   Kind in thought and deed; for He
   Sayeth, 'What ye do for others
   Ye are doing unto Me'.

128. Who can, what can?

Words and music: Betty Lou Mills

Chorus : Who can, what can? We can, you can.
Who can, what can? We can, you can.
Who can, what can? We can, you can,
We can serve the Lord.

1. Haven't got much money,
Haven't got much talent,
But the things we have got,
We will give to Him.
Chorus :

2. We may not be clever,
But we'll not say never;
With a cheerful heart, we'll
Do our best for Him.
Chorus :

129. Father, lead me day by day

Words: J. P. Hopps (d. 1912)

Music: ST. MARTIN   Mediaeval French Melody

1. Father, lead me day by day
   Ever in Thine own sweet way:
   Teach me to be pure and true,
   Show me what I ought to do.

2. When in danger, make me brave;
   Make me know that Thou canst save:
   Keep me safe by Thy dear side;
   Let me in Thy love abide.

3. When I'm tempted to do wrong,
   Make me steadfast, wise and strong;
   And when all alone I stand,
   Shield me with Thy mighty hand.

130. Joseph in Egypt

Words and music: Sister Oswin

1. Joseph had eleven brothers,
   And they wished him far away;
   Sold him as a slave into Egypt,
   For some silver coins one day.
   Chorus: He remembered the Lord in the land of Egypt
   And the Lord remembered him.

2. He worked very hard for his master,
   And was treated like a son,
   Until he was thrown into prison
   For a crime he hadn't done.
   Chorus:

3. He worked very hard for the warder
   And took care of all the men.
   He explained their dreams but he longed
   To have his freedom back again.
   Chorus:

4. Pharaoh had two dreams that bewildered him,
   Till Joseph made them plain.
   He was given power and appointed
   To take charge of all the grain.
   Chorus:

5. Joseph's brothers travelled to Egypt;
   Nowhere else could they buy bread.
   They didn't know this great man was Joseph,
   They were sure that he was dead.
   Chorus:

6. He discovered that they were sorry
   For their cruelty and greed;
   Told them who he was and forgave them,
   And he helped them in their need.
   Chorus:

131. Jesus, humble was your birth

Words: P. Appleford

Music: CATHERINE   F. G. Beaumont

1. Jesus, humble was Your birth,
   When You came from heaven to earth;
   Every day in all we do,
   Make us humble, Lord, like You.

2. Jesus, strong to help and heal,
   Showing that Your love is real;
   Every day in all we do,
   Make us strong and kind like You.

3. Jesus, when You were betrayed,
   Even on the Cross You prayed:
   Trusting in Your Father's care,
   Loving all men everywhere.

4. Jesus, risen from the dead,
   With us always, as You said;
   Every day in all we do,
   Help us live and love like You.

132. Here we come with gladness

Words: J. H. Johnston (d. 1908)　　　　　　　　　Music: OPPIDANS MEWS M. Shaw (d. 1958)

1. Here we come with gladness,
   Gifts of love to bring,
   Praising Him who loves us,
   Christ our Saviour King.

2. Small may be the offering,
   But the Lord will use
   Every gift we bring Him;
   None will He refuse.

3. More and more for Jesus
   May we gladly give;
   Giving, giving, giving,
   Is the way to live.

133. All that I have

Words and music: D. G. Montgomery

1. Two little fishes, five loaves of bread,
   Five thousand people by Jesus were fed.
   This is what happened when one little lad
   Gladly gave Jesus all that he had.

   Chorus: All that I have.
   All that I have.
   I will give Jesus all that I have.

2. One lonely widow, two coins small.
   Jesus was watching when she gave her all,
   And Jesus said, as His heart was made glad
   That she had given all that she had.

   Chorus: All that I have,
   All that I have,
   I will give Jesus all that I have.

134. Lord, here am I: send me

Words and music: H. W. Guinness

Mine are the hands to do the work;
My feet shall run for Thee;
My lips shall sound the glorious news:
Lord, here am I; send me.

135. The wise may bring their learning

Words: Book of Praise for Children, 1881, altd.

Music: Tyrolese Carol.

1. The wise may bring their learning,
   The rich may bring their wealth,
   And some may bring their greatness,
   And some their strength and health:
   We too would bring our treasures
   To offer to the King;
   We have no wealth or learning,
   What gifts then shall we bring?

2. We'll bring the many duties
   We have to do each day;
   We'll try our best to please Him,
   At home, at school, at play:
   And better are these treasures
   To offer to the King;
   Than richest gifts without them;
   Yet these we all may bring.

3. We'll bring Him hearts that love Him,
   We'll bring Him thankful praise,
   And lives for ever striving
   To follow in His ways:
   And these shall be the treasures
   We offer to the King,
   And these are gifts that ever
   Our grateful hearts may bring.

136. Lord Jesus, be Thou with us now

Words: W. F. B. Macalister (d. 1950)

Music: STELLA   Easy Hymn Tunes 1852

Capo behind 1st fret

Lord Jesus, be Thou with us now,
As in Thy house in prayer we bow;
And when we sing, and when we pray,
Help us to mean the words we say,
Help us to listen to Thy word,
And keep our thoughts from wandering, Lord.

137. In our work and in our play

Words: W. G. Wills (d. 1891)

Music: HARTS   B. Milgrove (d. 1810)

1. In our work and in our play,
   Jesus, ever with us stay;
   May we always strive to be
   True and faithful unto Thee.

2. May we in Thy strength subdue
   Evil tempers, words untrue,
   Thoughts impure and deeds unkind,
   All things hateful to Thy mind.

3. Jesus, from Thy throne above
   Do Thou fill us with Thy love,
   So that all around may see
   We belong, dear Lord, to Thee.

4. Children of the King are we,
   May we loyal to Him be:
   Try to please Him every day,
   In our work and in our play.

138. The King's highway

Music: Voke

Walking with Jesus, by His side I'll stay,
Walking with Jesus in the narrow way;
Travelling along together day by day,
Walking in the King's highway.

139. No, never alone!

Words and music: W. J. Kirkpatrick (d. 1921)

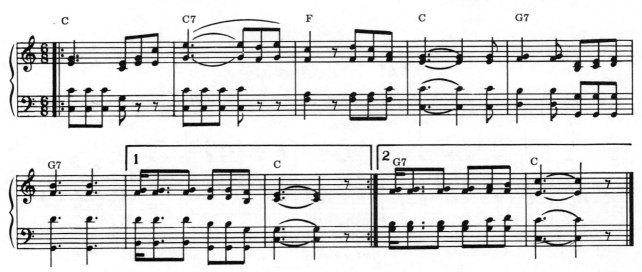

No, never alone,
No, never alone;
He promised never to leave me,
Never to leave me alone.
(Repeat)

140. Keep me shining, Lord

Words and Music: K. B. Wilkinson (d. 1928).

Keep me shining, Lord,
Keep me shining, Lord,
In all I say and do;
That the world may see Christ lives in me,
And learn to love Him too.

141. Trust and obey

Words: J. H. Sammis

Music: D. B. Towner

Trust and obey,
For there's no other way
To be happy in Jesus,
But to trust and obey.

142. Kept by the power of God

Words and music: W. J. Graham Hobson

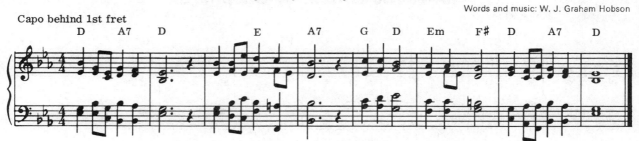

Kept by the power of God.
Kept by the power of God,
Day by day, come what may,
Kept by the power of God.

143. When the road is rough

Words and music: N. J. Clayton

When the road is rough and steep,
Fix your eyes upon Jesus,
He alone has power to keep,
Fix your eyes upon Him;

Jesus is a gracious Friend,
One on whom you can depend,
He is faithful to the end,
Fix your eyes upon Him.

144. The Lord's my Shepherd

Words: The Scottish Psalter 1650

Music: CRIMOND Melody J. S. Irivine (d. 1887)
Arr. T. C. L. Pritchard

1. The Lord's my Shepherd, I'll not want;
   He makes me down to lie
   In pastures green; He leadeth me
   The quiet waters by.

2. My soul He doth restore again;
   And me to walk doth make
   Within the paths of righteousness
   E'en for His own name's sake.

3. Yea, though I walk in death's dark vale,
   Yet will I fear none ill:
   For Thou art with me; and Thy rod
   And staff me comfort still.

4. My table Thou hast furnished
   In presence of my foes;
   My head Thou dost with oil anoint,
   And my cup overflows.

5. Goodness and mercy all my life
   Shall surely follow me;
   And in God's house for evermore
   My dwelling place shall be.

Arrangement by permission of Oxford University Press
This hymn may also be sung to the tune 'THE HAPPY WANDERER'

145. Surely goodness and mercy

Capo behind 1st fret

Words and Music: A. B. Smith and W. Peterson

Surely goodness and mercy shall follow me ⎫Repeat
All the days, all the days of my life. ⎭
And I shall dwell in the house of the Lord forever,
And I shall feast at the table spread for me;
Surely goodness and mercy shall follow me
All the days, all the days of my life,
All the days, all the days of my life.

146. The Lord's Prayer

Music: Traditional Arr. D. J. Crawshaw

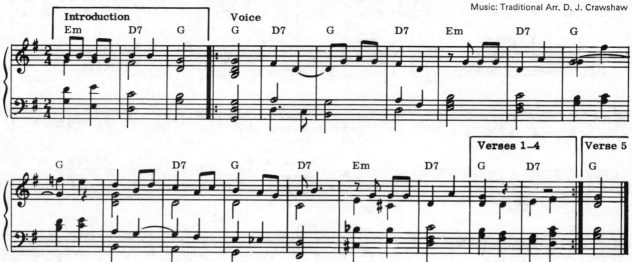

1. Our Father, who art in heaven,
   Hallowed be Thy name,
   Thy kingdom come, Thy will be done,
   Hallowed be Thy name.

2. On earth as it is in heaven,
   Hallowed be Thy name,
   Give us this day our daily bread,
   Hallowed be Thy name.

3. Forgive us all our trespasses,
   Hallowed be Thy name,
   As we forgive those who trespass against us.
   Hallowed be Thy name.

4. And lead us not into temptation,
   Hallowed be Thy name,
   But deliver us from evil
   Hallowed be Thy name.

5. For thine is the kingdom, the power and the glory,
   Hallowed be Thy name,
   For ever and ever, for ever, Amen.
   Hallowed be Thy name.

147. Kum ba yah

Words and Music: Traditional

1. Kum ba yah, my Lord, Kum ba yah.
   Kum ba yah, my Lord, Kum ba yah.
   Kum ba yah, my Lord, Kum ba yah.
   O Lord, Kum ba yah.

2. Someone's crying Lord, Kum ba yah.
   Someone's crying Lord, Kum ba yah.
   Someone's crying Lord, Kum ba yah.
   O Lord, Kum ba yah.

3. Someone's singing Lord, Kum ba yah.
   Someone's singing Lord, Kum ba yah.
   Someone's singing Lord, Kum ba yah.
   O Lord, Kum ba yah.

4. Someone's praying Lord, Kum ba yah.
   Someone's praying Lord, Kum ba yah.
   Someone's praying Lord, Kum ba yah.
   O Lord, Kum ba yah.

5. Hear our prayer, O Lord, hear our prayer,
   Keep our friends, O Lord, in Your care;
   Keep our friends, O Lord, in Your care.
   O Lord, hear our prayer.

148. Ask! Ask! Ask!

Ask! Ask! Ask! and it shall be given you;
Seek! Seek! Seek! and you shall find;
Knock! Knock! Knock! it shall be opened unto you,
Your Heavenly Father is so kind.
He knows what is best for His children,
In body, soul, and mind;
So ask! Ask! Ask! Knock! Knock! Knock!
Seek and you shall find.

149. For health and strength

Words: Traditional

Music: Melody from 'Graded Rounds and Catches'

For health and strength and daily food,
We praise Thy name, O Lord.

150. Our Father God, who gives to me

Words: C. Hardie

Music: BOYD   C. Hardie

1. Our Father God, who gives to me
   My ears to hear, my eyes to see,
   Help me to hear and see for Thee.

2. Our Father God, who gives to me
   My feet and hands, so strong and free,
   Help me to run and work for Thee.

3. Our Father God, who gives to me
   My voice, to laugh and shout with glee,
   Help me with joy to sing for Thee.

151. Thank You

Words: M. G. Schneider

Tr. and adapted. S. Lonsdale and M. A. Baughen

Music: M. G. Schneider Set out in key changes by D. G. Wilson

Capo behind 4th fret

1. Thank You for ev'ry new good morning,
   Thank You for ev'ry fresh new day,
   Thank You that I may cast my burdens
   Wholly on to You.

2. Thank You for ev'ry friend I have, Lord,
   Thank You for ev'ry one I know,
   Thank You when I can feel forgiveness
   To my greatest foe.

3. Thank You for leisure and employment,
   Thank You for ev'ry heartfelt joy,
   Thank You for all that makes me happy,
   And for melody.

4. Thank Your for ev'ry shade and sorrow,
   Thank You for comfort in Your Word,
   Thank You that I am guided by You
   Everywhere I go.

5. Thank You for grace to know Your gospel,
   Thank You for all Your Spirit's power,
   Thank You for Your unfailing love
   Which reaches far and near.

6. Thank You for free and full salvation,
   Thank You for grace to hold it fast.
   Thank You, O Lord I want to thank You
   That I'm free to thank!

We suggest, when accompanied by the guitar:
   1. All the verses are sung in one key.
   2. To achieve the same key changes as in the above music, slide the capo up one fret between verses.
   3. It may prove easier to move capo between alternate verses.

152. Stand up, stand up for Jesus

Words: G. Duffield (d. 1888)

Music: MORNING LIGHT G. J. Webb (d. 1887)

1. Stand up, stand up for Jesus,
   You soldiers of the cross!
   Lift high His royal banner,
   It must not suffer loss.
   From victory unto victory
   His army He shall lead,
   Till every foe is vanquished,
   And Christ is Lord indeed.

2. Stand up, stand up for Jesus!
   The trumpet call obey;
   Forth to the mighty conflict
   In this His glorious day.
   You that are men, now serve Him
   Against unnumbered foes;
   Let courage rise with danger,
   And strength to strength oppose.

3. Stand up, stand up for Jesus!
   Stand in His strength alone;
   The arm of flesh will fail you,
   You dare not trust your own.
   Put on the gospel armour,
   Each piece put on with prayer;
   Where duty calls or danger,
   Be never wanting there!

4. Stand up, stand up for Jesus!
   The strife will not be long;
   This day the noise of battle,
   The next the victor's song.
   To him that overcometh,
   A crown of life shall be;
   He with the King of Glory
   Shall reign eternally.

153. The Lord has need of me

Words and music: C. J. Allen

The Lord has need of me:
His soldier I will be;
He gave Himself my life to win,
And so I mean to follow Him,
And serve Him faithfully,
So, although the fight be fierce and long,
I'll carry on—He makes me strong;
And then one day His face I'll see,
And oh! the joy when He says to me,
'Well done! My brave Crusader!' (Alt. faithful servant).

154. Be thou strong

Covenanter Chorus

Words and music: J. H. Cansdale

Capo behind 1st fret

Be thou strong and very courageous,
For I have commanded thee.
Be not afraid,
Be not dismayed;
Thou shalt have victory.
I will be with thee, what-e'er betide,
Captain and Leader,
Friend and Guide.

155. He who would valiant be

Words: J. Bunyan (d. 1688)
Alt. P. Dearmer (d. 1936)

Music: MONKS GATE   from an English Traditional Melody
Coll., adpt. and arr. R. Vaughan Williams (d. 1958)

Capo behind 1st fret

1. He who would valiant be
   'Gainst all disaster,
   Let him in constancy
   Follow the Master.
   There's no discouragement
   Shall make him once relent
   His first avowed intent
   To be a pilgrim.

2. Who so beset him round
   With dismal stories,
   Do but themselves confound,
   His strength the more is.
   No foes shall stay his might,
   Though he with giants fight:
   He will make good his right
   To be a pilgrim.

3. Since, Lord, Thou dost defend
   Us with Thy Spirit,
   We know we at the end
   Shall life inherit.
   Then fancies flee away!
   I'll fear not what men say,
   I'll labour night and day
   To be a pilgrim.

From 'The English Hymnal' by permission of Oxford University Press

156. On the victory side

Words and music: W. J. Main

Capo behind 3rd fret

On the victory side,
On the victory side,
No foe can daunt me,
No fear can haunt me,
On the victory side.

On the victory side,
On the victory side,
With Christ within,
The fight we'll win,
On the victory side.

157. Be valiant, be strong!

Words and Music: E. H. G. Sargent (d. 1974).

Capo behind 1st fret

Be valiant, be strong,
Resist the powers of sin !
The fight is long, the foe is strong,
    but you shall win;
For through the power of Christ—
    the stronger than the strong—
You shall be more than conqueror,
Be valiant, be strong !

158. Onward, Christian soldiers

Words: S. Baring-Gould (d. 1924) Altd.

Music: ST. GERTRUDE A. S. Sullivan (d. 1900)

Capo behind 1st fret

Chorus

1. Onward, Christian soldiers,
   Marching as to war,
   Looking unto Jesus,
   Who is gone before :
   Christ, the royal Master,
   Leads against the foe ;
   Forward into battle,
   See His banners go !
Chorus : Onward, Christian soldiers,
   Marching as to war,
   Looking unto Jesus,
   Who is gone before.

2. At the name of Jesus,
   Satan's host doth flee ;
   On then, Christian soldiers,
   On to victory !
   Hell's foundations quiver
   At the shout of praise :
   Brothers, lift your voices ;
   Loud your anthems raise.
   Chorus :

3. Like a mighty army
   Moves the church of God :
   Brothers, we are treading
   Where the saints have trod :
   We are not divided,
   All one body we,
   One in hope and doctrine,
   One in charity.
   Chorus :

4. Crowns and thrones may perish,
   Kingdoms rise and wane,
   But the church of Jesus
   Constant will remain :
   Gates of hell can never
   'Gainst that church prevail ;
   We have Christ's own promise,
   And that cannot fail.
   Chorus :

5. Onward, then ye people,
   Join our happy throng ;
   Blend with ours your voices
   In the triumph-song ;
   Glory, praise, and honour,
   Unto Christ the King :
   This through countless ages
   Men and angels sing.
   Chorus :

159. There's a fight to be fought

Words and music: N. Pope

There's a fight to be fought, and a race to be run,
There are dangers to meet by the way;
But the Lord is my light and the Lord is my life,
And the Lord is my strength and stay.

On His Word I depend, He's my Saviour and Friend,
And He tells me to trust and obey;
For the Lord is my light, and the Lord is my life,
And the Lord is my strength and stay.

160. We are marching home

Words and music: M. J. H. Fox

Capo behind 1st fret

E A D G D Em A D

We are marching home to Heaven
In the army of our Lord;
And the shield of faith protects us
While the Bible is our sword.

When the march seems long
We can sing our song,
For our Saviour leads the way;
And the power of God the Spirit
Gives us strength to watch and pray.

© Scripture Union 1971

F. THE BIBLE

161. I am so glad

Words and music: P. P. Bliss Arr. E. M. Stephenson

I am so glad that our Father in heaven
Tells of His love in the Book He has given;
Wonderful things in the Bible I see;
This is the dearest, that Jesus loves me.

I am so glad that Jesus loves me,
Jesus loves me, Jesus loves me;
I am so glad that Jesus loves me,
Jesus loves even me.

© Music Arr. Scipture Union.

162. Make the Book live to me

Words and music: R. Hudson Pope (d. 1967)

Capo behind 1st fret

Make the Book live to me, O Lord,
Show me Thyself within Thy Word,
Show me myself and show me my Saviour,
And make the Book live to me.

163. Open my eyes

Words and music: E. H. Swinstead (d. 1976)

Capo behind 1st fret

Open my eyes, O Lord, to see
Wonderful things in Thy Word for me;
Ev'ry word is true and pure,

Ev'ry promise is tried and sure,
Lamp to my feet, and light on my way,
Guiding me safely to perfect day.

164. The sower

Words: R. Hawkins

Music: FROGGY WENT A-COURTIN' Traditional
Arr. E. M. Stephenson

1. The sower went out and spread the seed all around,
   The sower went out and spread the seed all around,
   The sower he spread that seed all around,
   He spread that seed all over the ground;
   The sower went out and spread the seed all around.

2. Now some of that seed fell down upon the way.
   Some of that seed fell down upon the way.
   Some of that seed fell upon the way
   And the birds came along and took it away;
   Now some of that seed fell down upon the way.

3. He watched that seed fall down on rocky ground,
   He watched that seed fall down on rocky ground,
   He watched it fall on rocky ground,
   It grew up quickly, but it soon fell down;
   He watched that seed fall down on rocky ground.

4. He watched it fall among some thistle weed,
   He watched it fall among some thistle weed,
   It fell among some thistle weed
   And grew, but the thistle choked that seed.
   He watched it fall among some thistle weed.

5. But some of that seed fell down upon good ground.
   Some of that seed fell down upon good ground,
   Some of that seed fell upon good ground,
   With lots of fruit it did abound,
   For some of that seed fell down upon good ground.

6. Now you can listen to the Word of God,
   You can listen to the Word of God,
   But if you listened all you could
   But bore no fruit it would do no good
   For you must act upon the Word of God.

165. For Your holy book we thank You

Words: R. Carter

Music: GOUNOD Harmony by F. Westbrook

1. For Your holy book we thank You,
   And for all who served You well,
   Writing, guarding and translating,
   That its pages might forth tell
   Your strong love and tender care
   For Your people everywhere.

2. For Your holy book we thank You
   And for those who work today,
   That the people of all nations,
   Reading it and following, may
   Know Your love and tender care
   For Your people everywhere.

3. For Your holy book we thank You,
   May its message be our guide,
   May we understand the wisdom
   Of the laws it will provide,
   And Your love and tender care
   For Your people everywhere.

166. The Bible tells of God's great plan

Music: ST. PETER   A. R. Reinagle (d. 1877)

1. The Bible tells of God's great plan
   For people everywhere,
   That all should learn to live in love
   And in His kingdom share.

2. He sent His Son, Lord Jesus Christ,
   To show His love for all,
   And many people followed Christ
   In answer to His call.

3. As God spoke then to men of old,
   So still He speaks today,
   We pray that we may learn His will
   And follow in His way.

167. The best book to read

Words: P. Bilhorn Adapted

Music: F. H. Ferrett Arr. Alastair Durden

The best book to read is the Bible,
The best book to read is God's Word.
If you read it every day
Then you'll know God's Way.
The best book to read is God's Word.

G. ALL GOD'S PEOPLE

168. Let all the world

Words: G. Herbert (d. 1633)

Music: LUCKINGTON B. Harwood (d. 1949)

Capo behind 1st fret

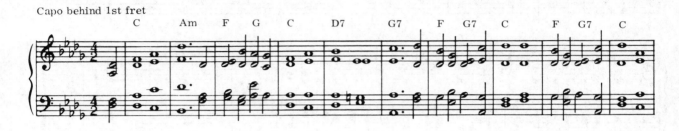

1. Let all the world in every corner sing,
'My God and King!'
The heav'ns are not too high,
His praise may thither fly :
The earth is not too low,
His praises there may grow.
Let all the world in every corner sing,
'My God and King!'

2. Let all the world in every corner sing,
'My God and King!'
The church with psalms must shout,
No door can keep them out:
But, above all, the heart
Must bear the longest part.
Let all the world in every corner sing
'My God and King!'

169. Remember all the people

Words: P. Dearmer (d. 1936)

Music: Tyrolese Carol

1. Remember all the people
   Who live in far off lands,
   In strange and lovely cities,
   Or roam the desert sands,
   Or farm the mountain pastures,
   Or till the endless plains
   Where children wade through rice fields
   And watch the camel trains:

2. Some work in sultry forests
   Where apes swing to and fro,
   Some fish in mighty rivers,
   Some hunt across the snow.
   Remember all God's children
   Who yet have never heard
   The truth that comes from Jesus,
   The glory of His Word.

3. God bless the men and women
   Who serve Him oversea;
   God raise up more to help them
   To set the nations free,
   Till all the distant people
   In every foreign place
   Shall understand His Kingdom
   And come into His grace.

170. Make it known!

Words and music: Ian Moore and Bill Simmons
Transcribed for piano by Garrett O'Brien

1. People coloured, people white,
   Far away and near,
   Need to know the love of God,
   Overcoming hate and fear.
   We must send the Good News out
   And help to make it known:
   God is love, and gave His Son,
   That His love might be shown.

2. Jesus came to a world of greed,
   And poverty and strife,
   That He might bring to everyone
   The gift of a fuller life.
   To love, to save, to teach, to heal,
   This is why He came.
   And He commands His followers now:
   'Go and do the same.'

3. To learn, to work, to pray, and give,
   This our part must be;
   That older people may go out
   Here and across the sea
   To heal the sick, to feed the poor,
   To help men sing God's praise.
   The work is hard, but Jesus says:
   'I am there always'.

4. He's with us now, as we play our part
   By doing all we can.
   He's with His messengers who preach
   About God's loving plan
   His love is shown where lame men walk.
   And the blind are made to see.
   'Inasmuch as you have done it,
   You have done it unto Me'.

171. Lift high the cross

Words: M. R. Newbolt based on G. W. Kitchin

Music: CRUCIFER S. H. Nicholson (1875-1947)

Chorus: Lift high the cross, the love of Christ proclaim,
Till all the world adore His mighty name.

1. Come, people, follow, where our Captain trod,
Our King victorious, Christ the Son of God:
Chorus:

2. From north and south, from east and west they raise
In growing unison their song of praise:
Chorus:

172. His own church

Words: Wilhelmenia D'A. Stephens

Music: STENKA RAZIN Traditional Melody
Arr. E. M. Stephenson

1. Long ago the friends of Jesus
   Who had lived with Him each day,
   Met together for His worship:
   Others followed in their way;

2. Bound together in one body,
   Jesus' friends the whole world o'er—
   His own church on His word founded—
   Him to honour evermore.

3. We would also strive to please Him,
   In His fellowship would live;
   So we band ourselves together.
   All our lives to Him to give;

4. Telling others of His goodness,
   Winning them to love Him too—
   His own church through all the ages,
   In the world His work to do.

INDEX OF FIRST LINES

INDEX OF FIRST LINES

INDEX OF FIRST LINES